THE OFFICE TRUTH,

FROM A TO Z,

UNDER DEEP CORPORATE COVER!

Sometimes, in the business world, people say what they mean. Sometimes they mean what they say. It doesn't matter which, if you have no idea what they're talking about.

Now at last, *Esquire* business columnist and irreverent wit Stanley Bing cracks the code of biz-speak. From mail room to boardroom, *BIZ WORDS* provides the secret key to successful office communication. Now you can pursue your career and *still* be your own person—as you play the corporate game with a secret grin!

"I HOPE THESE *BIZ WORDS* IMPACT ON YOUR CAREER IN THE NEAR AND INTERMEDIATE TERM AS YOU INTERFACE WITH YOUR COLLEAGUES, POSITION A VIABLE STANDING IN THE CORPORATE TREE, AND NETWORK YOUR WAY TO POWER, PRESTIGE AND UNNATURALLY EARLY RETIREMENT."

Stanley Bing

biz words

Power Talk for Fun and Profit

Stanley Bing

POCKET BOOKS

New York   London   Toronto   Sydney   Tokyo

An *Original* Publication of POCKET BOOKS

POCKET BOOKS, a division of Simon & Schuster Inc.
1230 Avenue of the Americas, New York, NY 10020

ISBN: 0-671-67414-5

First Pocket Books trade paperback printing May 1989

10 9 8 7 6 5 4 3 2 1

POCKET and colophon are trademarks of
Simon & Schuster Inc.

Printed in the U.S.A.

CONTENTS

220 Absolutely Indispensable Terms
No Serious Businessperson Can Do Without

Contents

Contents

Use 'Em and Abuse 'Em as You See Fit!

A NOTE ON WORDS

Throughout this glossary, reasonable people will notice the pronoun "he" used almost exclusively. This, naturally, creates the impression that women are nowhere to be found in the business cosmology, or that the strategies in this book apply to men only. Nothing could be further from the truth. There are many women in business, and they live and die by the same rules as do men. To avoid engorged constructions like "give him or her what he or she wants," however, the women in these pages will not be "she." And when I say "the guy sitting next to you," please accept the fact that he could be wearing a dress.

STANLEY BING

A

Acquisition could mean one of two things. (1) It could mean your company is moving aggressively into the future by gobbling up a lesser entity. An acquisition of this type can be small, affecting a tiny factory somewhere in the nation's heartland, or it can be an earthshaking event that blasts the lives of thousands. Whatever its size, it means opportunity for you, if you choose to seize it.

Just as William the Conquerer staffed his court with Normans, your people will invade the new organization and begin bossing fearful Saxons around. As a member of the dominant corporate culture, your aspirations and skills will carry a lot of weight. Go for the job you want in the new entity, and aim at least one title higher on the corporate ladder. Success in an acquired division is the closest thing to glory that corporate life can offer, especially to younger execs whose careers are still in development and who are willing to relocate. The new business was acquired to offer fresh blood to an organism that is ever aging and revivifying, and to build the bottom line. If you help make that happen, the kudos will resound where it counts.

(2) It could also mean *your* upcoming sale to a benevolent foreign power. If that's the case, get set to buckle down for a bumpy ride. Your people are no longer calling the shots. For a discussion on who will survive and who won't, see **Mergers.**

Administrative Assistant is the slave of top management and master of its existence. Though the administrative assistant usually looks, talks, and functions just as a normal secretary would, she (or occasionally he) is not. Sure, all the trappings of secretarial servitude are there—the typewriter, the boss's life in Week-At-A-Glance—but her real purpose is to grant or block access. There is no call, memo or buckslip that does not pass her desk, and she can move it at any speed she likes. That's why excellent relations with top management's administrative assistants is essential for the forward momentum of your projects and the growth of your career.

Simple politeness is often the most effective tool. Administrative assistants are a fiercely proud bunch, acutely aware of their proximity to both the lowest and the highest branches of the corporate tree. This double consciousness can make them very testy when they feel slighted. Treat them as individuals who have a tough job to do and they will repay you with loyalty and an almost conspiratorial willingness to get your agenda heard and dealt with. Treat them as functionaries and they will repay you in kind. Unless you enjoy waiting three weeks to get a four-minute meeting, you'll see the wisdom of cultivating an informal rapport with the tiger at the gates.

Agenda may be a formal rundown of any proceeding. But all communications between people have a hidden agenda, too, a complicated amalgam of needs, demands, and dreams that make all conversations, even in business, human. The heart of the unspoken agenda is simple, even childlike. Some people just want you to make them feel like a person. In that case, a little courtesy goes a long way. Others want you to direct them, and this, too, should be done, since there's no greater security than an army of dependents. Still others, usually senior managers or those who think they should be, carry around a complex unspoken agenda that craves obeisance. When necessary, this must be met before all others. But do so with subtlety, not oil, and assert your own program, too—it's part of what makes you tick, so don't abandon it. And do your best to keep the collective eye on the *spoken* agenda, the one that enumerates the business to be done. If you needed psychodrama, you could have stayed at home.

Aggravation, see Assholes.

Aggression is the fuel that most successful people need in order to dominate and conquer. The drive to go on the offensive is a definite asset and a necessary tool in your battle to get your ideas through a stubborn hierarchy. But a little aggression goes a long way, especially in a culture that values cooperation and team effort. The trick is to identify the acceptable mode of aggression in your company and stick to it. Like any other tool, it is useless, even self-destructive, if not used appropriately.

In the strategic planning departments of multinational corporations, for instance, the tone tends to be downright mellow. No steps are taken without deep and abiding consensus. For an impatient, high-pressure manager, the lethargic pace can be excruciating, the incessant meetings a colossal waste of wind and time. His colleagues may find him obnoxious, even jejune. Such a guy might be happier at a smaller, more entrepreneurial firm where no-nonsense guerrilla tactics are valued, even admired.

As always, a clear understanding of your culture will help direct your native aggressiveness. And keep in mind that one form of aggression is unacceptable in any culture: territorial encroachment.

Allies are colleagues who help you gain acceptance for your ideas and money for your projects. They should be carefully distinguished from friends, who are necessary for another purpose (see **Friendship**).

Allies do more than just say "Great idea!" when you float a notion in an open meeting—although that's a good start. They make sure you're included in important conversations and suggest you for tough assignments. In short, they do everything they can to build an important myth: that you're an indispensable part of the team and without you the forward momentum of the business would be compromised. Since your survival is almost always a direct function of your niche in the prevailing mythology, this is a very great service indeed. Without allies, a man is solitary, and for all but the heartiest, solitude breeds paranoia and failure. In fact, the only lone wolf in most corporations is the chairman.

You've got two responsibilities to your allies if you're to maintain them and increase their numbers. First, deliver the goods when your allies need you to—whether it involves writing a speech on short notice or producing a spread sheet in twenty-four hours. In other words, make them look good. Second, be loyal to your allies. This is easy when their stock is rising; loyalty becomes more difficult, but no less important, when eager birds are circling above their heads and the stench of decaying viability is in the air. For an examination of perhaps the most essential personal trait in business life, see **Loyalty.**

Ambition, at its worst, unalloyed with tact and displayed without shame, can be an ugly thing to see, turning haughty pillars of pin-striped dignity into wizened toadies bowing and scraping for a tasty tidbit from above. At its best, though, it is an expression of all that is hopeful and, ultimately, tragic about our circumscribed careers. Too much ambition is vulgar, like too many muscles, a tip-off that something tiny and vulnerable is cowering within. Too little, on the other hand, is disgusting. No one respects a guy without ambition.

The key, as always, is control. After all, ambition is just one of an arsenal of emotional weapons at your disposal. To let any one run amok is bad form. At one corporation, a sales and marketing director blew his career out of the water by chasing a promotion. He badgered the president, over and over again, demanding to know why he wasn't being selected. Finally, the president told him. It wasn't a happy meeting.

The highest form of ambition, the kind most valued by the eagles at the peaks of the aerie, is ambition for the corporation—its future, its culture, its profits—and you can't evince too much of that. The good soldier is still the heart of every company, and evident ambition for its welfare is the best evidence that a man is one with his organization, and that his fate is safe within its walls.

Anger can be good for you, since every self-respecting person in a corporation knows you have to be a schmuck not to feel it often and express it upon occasion. The business world is just like life, filled, aside from its wonders, with little things that bother you—injustice, dishonesty, stupidity, greed, incompetence, sloth, venality, and reamed-out budgets. If you don't feel anger, for example, when your company lays off seventy people and then goes right out and throws a lavish Christmas bash, something is wrong with you. Choose the time and place for your display of pique, however, since some top execs can handle subordinates in a rage and others can't. And don't step over the line into insubordination.

Do what you can to turn the anger into a concrete demand—for a new title, a new office, retribution, or change. And bide your time.

Appointments are made to be kept, except, perhaps, with friends, who can be offended without fear of reprisal. The problem is that one's enthusiasm for an upcoming appointment often ends precisely three hours before it's to occur. It's a lot easier to look forward to a breakfast meeting with your public relations consultant than to actually endure it; and a working lunch at your desk, behind your comfy door, can seem like paradise next to short ribs and stiff chat with the director of training. Worse, as essentially frivolous appointments loom on your calendar, the actual business of the day always moves in and crushes your face. An ort of information demanded by the executive suite may suddenly loom a lot larger than the power lunch you were planning with your equipment supplier. So be frugal in making your appointments. They could turn out to be a pain in the ass later on.

And if you have to break an appointment, don't be afraid to lie. People appreciate the effort. "I just got called into a crucial meeting with the chief executive officer and I'll probably be here until midnight," makes a canceled vendor feel better than "I'm a basket case and I just can't stand the idea of meeting you for drinks after work to discuss digital vacuum cleaners." Don't forget to use the telephone call in which you cancel to make a future appointment you fully intend to keep. Don't, however, under any circumstances, say, "Let's have lunch." People may think you're insincere.

Arrivals and Departures are like the first and last moves in any game—play them well if you expect to win. Unless you're cultivating a reputation for eccentricity, or out to score a power point at someone else's expense, get where you're going on time. Nothing inflames other large egos more than having to cool their heels waiting for your agenda to get rolling. It implies your concerns are greater than theirs, your time more valuable. Maybe that's true, but why rub it in? If you don't watch out, people will start arriving late to *your* meetings, even canceling them altogether with an aplomb approaching spite. So get there, and use your arrival to make an entrance. In some cases, this means little more than a solemn nod to a roomful of mummies. Other times you'll want a big, splashy entrance that cracks everybody up—a lusty ejaculation of the word "Coffee!" accompanied by an expression of good-humored but extreme distress can totally poleax a morning meeting for instance. Whatever you do, make people sort of happy to see you.

And when you gotta go, do so, except when you're at a compulsory event from which people are only excused by the chairman or death. Be aware that moments of departure are unstructured. People feel just a little more human, less functionalized, and it's easy to let your guard down on the way out the door and pass an inappropriate remark to a crusty superior, push a project just a little too hard out of sheer excess adrenaline, or, worse, find yourself saddled with a last-minute good idea from a honcho who likes to give orders on the way back to his office. Of course, exits are also rife with possibilities. A good endgame can breed the kind of informality in which friendships and alliances are formed. A comradely arm on the vice-president of marketing's elbow after he gave a presentation can earn you three lunches with a whole new crowd.

Ass-Covering is a craft, not an art. There's nothing pretty or elegant about it, so don't be embarrassed to go about protecting your keester with vigor and, when necessary, ferocity. Often the best medium for self-perpetuation is paper, produced before, not after, the fact. Make a habit of documenting situations that have a scent of peril about them, the projects your

sixth sense tells you could stink up later. Any interview with
the media, for example, in which you said "no comment,"
should be chronicled, as should a meeting where you feel
bad decisions were made. Just listen to your paranoia talking
—it's probably right.

When the worst happens, produce your evidence and make
your case. Don't apologize for anything until you feel comfortable with the level of blame—if any—that is being attached to
you. Then beg pardon for anything you feel bad about, but
nothing more. Of course, there are times when you've got to
crawl back into favor. For a discussion of that fine art, see
Screwing Up.

Assholes. God must have loved them, He made so many.
The species comes in an assortment of sizes and varieties, and
each must be dealt with properly, some with finesse, others
with savagery. Assholes make life aggravating by blocking
projects through inaction, squabbling over turf, grabbing
credit and shuffling blame, and otherwise mixing business with
neurosis. All are nerds, in one way or another, but only mean
nerds are genuine assholes (see **Nerds**).

• *Jerks* generally stand in your way more out of stupidity
than malice—though that's often there, too—but aggressive
dumbness doesn't have to be malicious to be a pain in the neck.
Be nice to jerks, preen them, and they'll reward you with a
stupid kind of loyalty that is just as useful as the more elevated
sort.

• *Schmucks* are nasty jerks. A real schmuck would piss on
your parade simply because it makes his day. At heart, they
hate people with lots of good ideas and abundant energy, and
will do everything they can to shut them down. That's because
they are acutely aware they have neither, a painful realization
that could turn anyone into a schmuck. So treat them with
mercy, when you can, but if one starts pulling your chain, come
down hard. Yelling works, so does excluding them from crucial
meetings and reprimanding them in writing, with copies to all.
There's nothing a true schmuck respects more than someone
willing to provide him with the abuse he deserves.

• *Bastards,* on the other hand, must be watched with care,

and cultivated. If a lot of your friends are bastards, you're probably doing all right, for they make mighty rotten enemies. Bastards were born mean, and rejoice at other people's misfortunes. The only people they like are those whom they identify with their own survival and success, and even those . . .

So steer clear of altercations with them, and don't be queasy about showing some respect. Of course, if you're a little bit of a bastard yourself, do your best to give as good as you get. It's more fun, and if you win a couple of battles you may find an unexpected ally, because, unlike schmucks, they favor not abuse but a thorough asskicking followed by drinks. Once a former adversary starts supporting you, it's amazing how your feelings about him will change.

• *Pricks* must be destroyed, blasted from the corporation without a trace. Whatever you can do is fair game. If it sounds like there's a personal dimension to this, you're right, because a fellow human being becomes a three-dimensional prick only when he, or she, is after *you,* torpedoing your plans, slandering you in your absence, revealing unwise confidences you might have dropped into his hands, stealing projects from your control, and otherwise placing your career in jeopardy. Unfortunately, pricks are almost always more powerful than you—if they weren't, they'd just be jerks. Do your work, plan, and wait. And use the time to develop your defenses. For a discussion of this campaign, see **Power Base.**

Ass-Kissing is addictive, and, like junkies, ass-kissers are often found in packs, nodding. They also tend to attach themselves to guys whose egos are diseased, whose image of themselves is either so dwarfed or gigantized it needs constant fuel for the hard work it has to do. That is ass that will always need kissing, and a more boring and fearful occupation is unknown to man, or woman either. Of course, when you're around one of the preeners, you'll probably have to spew a little flattery about. They expect it, and feel hurt when you don't offer it. So it's best to absent yourself from their company altogether, when feasible. That's what phones are for. Try to associate with people whose ego is strong enough to kiss itself.

B

Backstabbers can be neutralized, but you've got to be able to identify them first. This can be difficult. They stab backs, don't they?

You can spot a backstabber quite easily, however, if you read the signs before he targets you. He's the one who's usually in the process of publicly sautéeing one lame duck or another. Today, it's the vice-president of finance, who spilled drawn butter on his bib at the corporate picnic, ha-ha-ha. Tomorrow, it's you, who blew a major presentation to the administration council, supposedly. Word of mouth in a company creates its own kind of truth, turning illusion into reality faster than you can say "not viable." Worse, backstabbers since Cassius have found comfort in numbers, especially when blood has been drawn. So look for a bunch of muttering guys with a lean and hungry look. And steer clear.

Protect yourself, too, with a thick armor of friends and spies. Keep one another informed of negative vibes in the air, especially those that may be reaching the ear of top management. When all else fails, invite the backstabber to your office and make him stab you in the face. That takes something he lacks: guts. And there's no law against besmirching his name when you have the chance. Two can play that game.

Beancounters are the invisible men who crank out the numbers and take the money to the bank. They see revenue, profit, depreciation, amortization, and taxes not as inert lines on green paper, but as the throbbing heart of the enterprise. They're right. Even though a corporation is people, a product, an image, a culture, at its core it is nothing but money. Those are the beans beancounters count.

When young, beancounters may appear to be drones. They dress like moderately successful undertakers and converse like Buddhas. In later life, because they tend to be even-tempered, patient, and savvy, and have kept on buzzing while thousands of fireflies have perished, they may inherit great position and power. So don't be too snooty with the quiet men. They may be keeping score, as usual.

Blame is like a collect phone call—maybe you accept it, maybe you don't. When a project was blown because you couldn't meet a deadline, for instance, you'll probably have to eat some dirt. It's also wise to make amends when one of the mighty is peeved with you. One apology is worth twenty good excuses when you're being reamed by a guy who is more interested in collecting scalps than assessing responsibility. Other times, though, refuse it. When you didn't produce a report that was never assigned, or lost a deal because headquarters didn't get you the signature in time, don't grovel, just state the facts. Of course, if you're wrong, you're dead meat and a schmuck to boot. But if you're wronged, a little righteous indignation may make your critic think twice and come to a new conclusion.

Boardroom is the most beautiful and formal place in the corporation, the site of its most hallowed rituals. Before a major meet, with the holy-of-holies poised in austere finery, the boardroom glows with all that is eternal, dignified, and elegant about business. It is a place of power, and right action within its confines is mandatory. Dress for it, when you go. No shirt-sleeves, no penny loafers, unless it's an impromptu gathering. A dark suit with a whisper of pinstripe is always a good bet, but if your corporate culture is more hang-loose, costume yourself to the limits of conservatism. A bit of additional formality, too, in your salutations, adds to the sense of mutual importance the room provides. If there's food or coffee, which there generally is, try to keep your chin clean. When the time comes to get down to work, of course, play your game. But be aware that every word, every gesture, in fact, is slightly heightened, more in focus. A well-played hand in the boardroom sticks with you, makes you a contender for further matches. A nerdy or outlandish move could mark you for life.

Boonies are any towns smaller than yours. It's natural to feel a little supercilious about people there; they dress differently, seldom use terms like "interface" and "excellence," and consistently spend less than thirty dollars for lunch. Resist the temptation to look down your nose at the boonies, however. There isn't a product (except, perhaps, for pastrami) that isn't sold there, and it's very often where the actual revenue engines of a company lie. The corporate headquarters of a textile firm may be in midtown Manhattan, for instance, but its wage slaves are in South Carolina, with distributors at every stop from Maine to Maui. So don't be too smug about your corporate status when you interface with the boonies. And if you work out in the boonies, be proud. Quite a few backwoods boys are shaking the trees in Manhattan these days, snapping up undervalued companies, toting their merged assets back to the wilds of Oklahoma, Kansas, Georgia, and Tennessee.

Boss is the person you report to, but your boss's boss is also your boss, as is your boss's boss's boss. In fact, anyone with a superior title who would like to tell you what to do could be your boss, if you let him. This can lead to problems, especially if the work he assigns takes you far afield from your department. Remember that your only genuine responsibility lies with your direct reporting relationship. When push comes to shove, only he (or she) is your master, and only to him, and the company itself, do you owe absolute fealty. This doesn't mean you don't do everything within your power to please all the birds on the corporate tree, but your boss is your guru, and, many times, trouble for him means trouble for you. So even if he's a jerk, hang in there. Your boss may be all you have to protect you when a storm breaks.

There is one major exception to this approach. When your boss is whirling in concentric circles down the corporate drain, swim as fast as you can in the opposite direction. Continue to take orders, naturally, and perform with your customary excellence. And be nice. But begin to serve a wider range of masters, and to make your presence known to other, more secure nabobs. This will be considerably easier if you have already developed a reputation for solid work and independence. When your boss finally does disintegrate, labor with ferocious zeal to win over your new one, to become part of his team. A new boss is looking for allies and support, and there is no more welcome place to find it than right next door in a smaller office.

You may also find yourself filling your former boss's shoes—and sitting behind his desk as well. This may inspire a pang of guilt, but don't take that too seriously. After all, life goes on. Within you and without you.

Bottom Line in any business is performance—operational, personal, and financial. Delivering the goods—on time and under budget—is the single most important criterion by which you'll be judged. The rest—style, culture, politics, relationships, lunching, brunching, dining, whining—is icing on the cake.

Brainstorming is a highly valued activity, especially in fields where ideas are commodities. Advertising, for instance, leans heavily on collective inspiration. It's lonely work, trying to come up with a new way of selling toilet paper by yourself. Actually, there really isn't a serious project around that can't benefit from a little healthy confab among interested parties.

Brainstorming can be a lot of fun when the stakes aren't too high—a chance to put your feet up on the conference table, drink free soda, and make a few friends. A real bond is forged between good brainstormers. They see each other put forth stupid ideas, have a couple of laughs at each other's expense, and generally learn to value each other's creativity, individuality, and team spirit.

Bogus brainstorming, on the other hand, occurs when self-promoting jerks with no ideas at all are called together to share them ad nauseam, or when no single individual has the will, power, or guts to formulate the gooey, shapeless mess that brainstorming creates into a coherent plan. In short, no work gets done, leaving everyone enervated. Such meetings are worse than useless, because good ideas—always in short supply—are wasted. If you cannot absent yourself from the felicities on these occasions, withdrawal into a shell is effective. Try a little polite doodling (the company logo is a perfect and appropriate subject anytime). It sends the message that you have real work to do. You have, right? And if you're not invited to the next pointless windstorm, so much the better for you.

Breakfast Meetings can be delicious opportunities to cut through the clutter and get some business done before others do. Don't eat a big meal the night before, and get some sleep. Showing up with valises under your eyes and slurping down nothing but black coffee says something bad about you, so dress sharp, eat with gusto, and make the breakfast fun. As at any meeting, make sure you know the agenda beforehand and get it taken care of—but remember that the unspoken subtext of any breakfast is cordiality, even affection. When you're invited to take the most important meal of the day with someone, it means that person doesn't mind seeing your face first thing in the morning. Keep it that way.

Briefcase is like a pocket handkerchief—part necessity, part affectation. In many cultures, it's an essential prop without which you will not be taken as a serious player. In such places you're apt to see a range of ostentatious and capacious briefcases, each suited to the pretensions of the man, from junior executives with crisp attaché boxes to senior management with the corporate equivalent of ghetto blasters. Many more youthful firms, however, are getting lean in briefcase attire as they are in all aspects of managerial style, and suitcases filled with the bulky detritus of months of projects and schemes are frowned on as proof of dinosaur status. Look about you, and while doing your best (as always) to adhere to the prevailing wisdom, do the minimum. People respect a guy who can think on his feet without sorting through the dusty relics of past correspondence. Get what you need and leave the rest.

Brushing Off persistent suitors can be an unavoidable corollary of your power and success, but do it with gentleness and tact. You could be—and probably have been—in the poor schmuck's shoes, so try exercising a little common humanity before you get out your big broom and send the person hurtling out of your life. Some methods that precede brutality are:

• *Rescheduling:* Everything has remained jocular, and the pretense of future intercourse survives. But once you've postponed that lunch seven times, or been unable to nail down that informal drinks date for two years, the guy should get the message. If he doesn't, try:

• *Begging Off:* This is an extremely polite way of saying no. In fact, you're doing just that, but not yet putting it into words. Most intelligent people will take, "I can't really see getting together for the next six months. Call me then," as a courteous indication you're not interested. When they don't, there's always:

• *Unavailability:* A little more callous, but by now you probably feel he deserves it. Have your secretary screen your calls with a vengeance, and don't return the unwanted entreaty. Best excuse: "He's in a meeting but I'll have him get back to you right away." Then don't. For those for whom only the worst will do, you'll have to employ:

• *The Kiss-off:* The fact that you're using this method means you never want to see the joker again, so get the job done and make it short and sweet. Don't scream and don't lose your temper, but make your point and leave no crack through which the worm can wriggle back.

And if *you* are getting a brush-off after your best efforts, act sharp and take a powder. A rejection accepted with class maintains your dignity, and there's no reason why you can't come back in a couple of months to see if the weather has cleared. Who knows, somewhere down the road the guy may be in the market for what you're pitching. And if he's not, screw him.

Buckslips are God's answer to memos. They're the little scraps of formal paper—usually with the company logo and your name and title attached—that pass along a document and the responsibility to act on it to the next available party. Make sure you have an ample supply at hand, and use them whenever you have to attach your name to something in transit. They can be typed and signed, or dashed off with a Flair, but don't load them down with decision points—that's not what they're for. And don't send them fluttering off on their own, either, unbacked by any attachments; they're too flimsy. Buckslips weren't designed to convey insight, wit, or large amounts of information, but to deliver a simple message: "I took care of this. Now what are you going to do about it?" Isn't that what passing the buck is all about?

Budgeting is a creative activity, akin to the writing of fiction. Don't let all the dry columns and numbers fool you: behind the facade of scientific organization, a budget is nothing more or less than a passionate exercise in self-justification and an assertion of your priorities. If the corporation believes in you, it should put its money where its mouth is, and that means dough for you. Don't pad your budget, however, with outlandish demands; just make sure you have a line for every project or expense you can justify.

A good budget should contain two things: room for activity and growth, and the illusion of leanness. You can achieve this by packing your budget with many discrete entries, each pared down to reasonable size, each expendable only at great peril to the well-being of the firm. And, if the worst should come to pass and one or two are cut during budget review, so what? You've still got the massive edifice of your good ideas standing proud and tall after the whittling.

Of course, if push is coming to shove in your corporation and creative ideas are less important than financial survival, get with the program and ream out your budget along with the rest. Nothing is more aggravating to expense choppers than executives who refuse to bite the bullet. When the ship is going down, it's stupid to try to save the deck chairs. And, when the budget process is over, declare victory and live within your means. Hopefully you'll be around next year to push those numbers through again.

Burnout is a passé concept of the late 1970s. The idea was that fast-track players reached a certain point in their careers when, like a bad reactor, they melted down from a combination of neglect, boredom, pressure, and an overload of poisonous materials. This is hogwash. If you've chosen the right line of work, and you take your vacations seriously, you should be able to go on with zest as long as you're promoted. And that's the key. Genuine burnout—a feeling of torpor and muffled hostility toward the entire culture—arises from career stagnation. When you feel unmotivated for more than a month (anything less should be ignored as merely part of being a wage slave), or are attacked by existential angst more than once a quarter, start looking at the world outside your door. You'll be surprised at the sudden rush of energy that comes from new challenges.

Business Cards should be carried on your person, but don't overuse or overvalue them. Only salespeople really need them all the time. That's because it's generally up to the person who is seeking business to initiate the transfer of identities. So if you're the one who's being petitioned, wait for your suitor to present his card, then, and only then, offer yours in return. If you're the one who is on the make, wait until the end of the confrontation to flash your particulars. A card should simply be a memory-jogger, building on the positive impression you've created with your energy, charm, and style. Don't make it carry any more weight than that.

Busywork is all the witless stuff you've got to do just because your boss tells you to—those projects that arise out of a fevered executive brain and should by all rights have remained there. Unfortunately, senior managers have enthusiasms and whims just like normal people, and a fleeting notion is just a breath away from a fiat to a master delegator. This interface between impulse and demand can magically engender meaningless work for subordinates all the way up and down the reporting structure.

The trick is to divine whether the inane directive is a passing fancy or an idée fixe. A good amount of busywork will simply go away after a dose of sheer, crushing procrastination. When your boss asks you, "What's happened to the Strategic Mission Test Module, anyway?" you should be able to cite a dozen projects that—by mutual agreement—need attention first. If a job remains on a back burner for long enough, it's bound to leave the mind of the average manager. On the other hand, the *president's* pet plan for Organizational Quality Control and Employee Ascertainment should be executed soon after the second request for it. A little busywork delivered to the right party never hurt anyone's career, especially if the work was done well and granted a respect it didn't deserve.

Buzzer is a device on an intercom that alerts you to the fact that you have a call, or your boss wants you, or a peer needs consultation. Whatever it means, it's almost always an intrusion. It's mighty annoying to have a four-party, transcontinental phone hookup on hold while your secretary, having insistently buzzed, tells you on the intercom that she's going to take a walk in the park because it's so beautiful outside. Use your buzzer when you mean it. Until then, keep it sheathed.

Buzzwords are culture-specific terms whose use confers instant membership in the corporate club. Suppose your business is concerned with providing the tiny chromium nipples that connect hydroelectric transformers. When these objects wear out, they are said to "spear." One Friday, a senior officer

says, "Boy, I'm speared," at the end of a long meeting. By next
Monday, it's being used throughout the firm, and one person
uses it in an interview with a trade publication. Two weeks
later, it appears in *USA Today*. A buzzword has been born, and
will live as long as there is one person who has not heard it.
Pick up current buzzwords and enjoy them, within reason. But
don't get too attached. Singing the newest tune is part of keeping up with the pack. For a discussion of the magnificent
language of which buzzwordery is merely a part, see **Jargon.**

Capital is any form of wealth that's utilized to produce more wealth, any asset the corporation calls its own (including you) that can be boiled down to make money breed more of itself. Because that's really what capital is: money, pure and simple. The word "money," however, when used in business discourse, has a plebeian, inelegant, inexact ring to it. Crass, even. "We need to shell out a lot more money on this project or we'll have to shut it down," sounds so much less elevated than, "We'll have to requisition additional capital expenditures or terminate operations." So whenever a financial type begins to bandy about the term—as in capital project, capital gains, capital investment, etc.—just think bucks. And you can take that to the bank.

Capitalism is an economic system in which the means of production are owned by private individuals and corporations (and their stockholders). These relatively few individuals share in "profits" and employ the majority of citizens, retaining their services for what are known, among other things, as "wages." Profits seem to mount a lot faster than wages. Thus, capitalism appears to come most highly recommended by those in the first category. You may try to join their ranks, but be warned. You'll probably labor your whole life, make a good (even bodacious) living, attain considerable power and standing, and still remain a wage slave. It takes dedication, entrepreneurial spirit, sagacious investment, and luck to escape slave status. After all, you weren't born to great influence and power, or you probably wouldn't be reading this book—you'd be clipping coupons and politely lunching investors.

Cigarettes are a filthy, immature, self-destructive habit that many people love very much and cannot do without. If you smoke, do not do so around people who hate the smell of it and have contempt for those weak and pathetic souls who haven't got the will to toss their butts away. Abstinence is most crucial at large staff meetings where the corporate hierarchy does not indulge and there are no ashtrays. At such gatherings, puffing on a nail is about as attractive, and noticeable, as hauling out a hypo and mainlining a hit of horse. Smoke where you can do so without provoking the narrowing of eyes and clucking of tongues. Aggressive smoking in an unfriendly environment is no fun. It also shows an embarrassing lack of self-control on your part, a bad message to convey in any company. It's also rude.

If you do not smoke, however, don't be so damned smug. Don't you have any vices? Don't you swill too much free Scotch at office parties, or ostentatiously order Perrier-with-kiwi on a date when club soda will do, or eat too many saturated fats? If you have no vices, congratulations—you're really obnoxious.

Corporations, like collectives, are amalgams of all sorts of otherwise incompatible individuals, all laboring for the common glory of the enterprise. So peace between breathers and smokers should be struck as emblematic of the kind of broad cooperation that makes a team work.

Client is anyone to whom you provide service. In advertising or retailing, of course, the client relationship is clear—I sell, you buy. Within a company, however, and in all disciplines, it's useful to establish who is the client and who the provider, even if the only payment is respect. The corporate speech writer's client is the guy who calls one morning and yammers, "I have to talk to three hundred and fifty Rotarians tomorrow! Help!" To the regional controller, it's the field location that requests fourteen permutations of the quarterly budget to find out where the cash flow has agglutinated. Once the basic contract between provider and client is established, it's incumbent upon them both to live up to it. Naturally, the former must deliver the goods. But clients who change the order in midstream, or who don't provide adequate information (or funds) for the task, are dooming the project to failure. In this association, as in all others, success lies in synergy.

Cliques exist in every collection of more than three people. Try not to belong to them. By their very nature, they are unkind and exclusionary. Develop friendships instead. They stand up a lot better under stress than cliques, which are based on mutual anxiety and cowardice and tend to evaporate when you need them most.

Coffee is not really an issue in a happy work environment, but in a shop where secretaries get no respect it can become an angry deadlock between middle management and its serfs. The fact is: secretaries should get your coffee unless they are busy and you are not. The arguments against this revolutionary statement are as follows:

- It's a degrading task, not worthy of my skills.
- It is not part of my job description.
- It's sexist.

Rebuttals

- Tough. Everyone in business performs futile, boring, and menial tasks when politely ordered to do so. This is the basis of all reporting structures. Those who refuse or, worse, grumble, may justly be whipped for insubordination. It's not uncommon for senior vice-presidents to sharpen the chairman's pencil; your secretary can make your life easier, too, within reason. That's her (or his) job, as much as typing and filing.

• Okay. I'll make it a part of your job description. In writing, if necessary.

• It is not. Arrogant, perhaps. Lazy. Even childish. But not sexist. The average executive would send an armadillo to get his or her coffee. And that's not humanist.

Company Car, see Perks.

Competition is the hotwire that jumpstarts the corporate machine, nothing more. Certainly, the collective impulse to crush the opposition can provide a little extra juice, but fellows who say things like, "Let's win this one for the chairman" receive unkind stares in all but the most banal organizations. Corporations, after all, are not the Green Bay Packers, and a little rah-rah Lombardi-ism goes a long way when there's an important team effort on and the stakes are grim. Too, competition between peers often turns a working environment into a dangerous cesspool of Machiavellian kidney punching. Managers who foster such fruitless competition in their lower ranks leave a train of career destruction in their wake.

A private competitive streak, on the other hand, in which victory and loss are registered on an internal scale, is at the heart of success. That's the battle between each man and his sense of destiny. No matter how misplaced and self-aggrandizing that personal myth may be, it's the path to right action. So keep your competition to yourself. At least if you fall on your face, your audience will be limited to your biggest fan.

Compromise, unless you're an insecure wonk, should be easy. Indulge in it prodigally as long as the stakes are low. The effect of being known as a good compromiser can be immeasurably more valuable to you in the long run than being renowned for unbending integrity. Remember that business is one of the most complicated mechanisms in creation, with thousands of separate variables determining the success of the whole. You cannot possibly be aware of all these factors, nor have a hint, no matter how effective you may be in your small corner, of how to control the big picture. So listen to what other people have to say, allow your positions to shape themselves gradually, and don't set up any big confrontations that aren't amenable to a little healthy positional give and take.

There are times, without question, not to compromise. For a discussion, see **Kicking Ass.**

Computers are everything humanity is not—obedient, efficient, silent, and fast. This makes them good partners and excellent lunch companions. People who resist computerization are shutting themselves away from a powerful business tool that takes the rote out of writing and the crunch from the numbers game. Computers also cancel the ill effects of inept secretarial support—since there's no mistake that cannot be eradicated by a quick eye and a flick of a blip.

Those who can should aggressively get with the program. Learn to file, process words, iterate spread sheets, or perform other essential and noxious daily chores electronically. Don't bother to learn a new procedure until you need it in your work; then absorb it the way you did ninth-grade algebra—through boring, crushing repetition and practice. You'll be glad you did. It will help organize you, reduce paper glut, and most importantly, give you more time to think. That's one human function computers cannot yet replace.

Conference Call, see Squawkbox.

Conformity is the best policy. Obvious nonconformists are the mayflies of corporate life, doomed to live but for one incandescent moment, then to disappear into the ether. Some are brilliant losers unable to communicate their ideas to the tribe. Others are plain old-fashioned losers whose careers are a mystery to all who find these omnipresent bummers in their midst. All are distinguished by the inability to meld into the culture and be unseen when necessary. They stick out in spite of all attempts to do otherwise, and when the fur begins to fly, they are, inevitably, the first ones skinned.

That said, note that there is usually a range of acceptable conformity within which a relatively wide range of behavior is tolerated. To enjoy the greatest latitude, conform to the costume. Be it crisply starched white shirts and blue serge suits, jeans and corduroy sportcoats, Ban-Lon jumpsuits and coke spoons, don the requisite threads and join the party. Anyone who has ever seen a corporate executive in Bermuda shorts knows how much clothes can make the man.

Don't, however, under any circumstances, forfeit your sense of who you are and how you have to play the game in order to do your best. The most successful businesspeople are 100 percent *themselves* all the time. For further discussion, see **Style.**

Consultants generally make a lot of money for very little work. While inside droids slave away over hot Wangs for reasonable wages, ladling out paperwork and sweating bullets over details, consultants float above like angels, or vultures. Many carve a career out of taking meals, tossing out good ideas over eggs and bacon, pastrami on rye, and steak au poivre with equal abandon. Others breeze into a troubled environment, help sweep a few bleeding corpses out the door, collect their fee, and move on. Still others haul down massive monthly retainers for a periodic six-page memo suggesting some more things for the staff to do. When they are bad, they are very, very bad, and aggravating to work with, too.

When they are good, however, they shine. Since the good consultant has no ultimate responsibility to anything but his own professionalism, he's comfortable looking at the warts and arthritic joints of the corporation, the things no one from within could see. He then goes about helping people on the inside find some answers for themselves.

If you find a consultant within your midst, do the obvious—take him to lunch and let him consult. Plumb his hidden agenda, too. A consultant always plugs a hole. Make sure it's not yours. If you find he is supposed to provide a service to you, make him work. If he doesn't, and isn't servicing anyone so's you'd notice, get him canned. He's sucking off money that could be spent for a staff person, one dedicated to the life of the group, who could be paid less to do more, who could, in short, be given a job.

Contract, spoken or not, exists between any two people doing business together. Make sure that, no matter its formality, an agreement on dates, rates, and responsibilities is reached in all your doings. It's especially best to get unspoken contracts out in the open. That way, everyone knows what's expected and who to blame when it doesn't get done.

Conventions are a chance to kick out the jams, but don't make a jerk of yourself. It's easy to. The liquor is omnipresent and sometimes free. You're away from home, and in strange surroundings to say the least, since conventions are often held in big cities with lots to offer. Cities like Las Vegas.

The temptation to mutate into a wild party animal may be overpowering. By all means make sure you know whom you're misbehaving with, and get as much dirt on him as he's getting on you. That way you'll have a wealth of "Christ was I drunk last week" jokes to share at the postmortems and you'll both feel safe behind the other's paranoia.

Conventions also offer a prime means of networking and finding new jobs. Just be aware that the plump nabob you're courting may be grasping at straws himself.

Finally, if you're happy at home and haven't really got anything to sell, if you don't really feel like getting loaded in a strange hotel among insincere people, stay back at the plant, man the phones, listen to the hiss of the sound-masking system, and take a few liquid lunches of your own.

Conversation is not simply cheap in business, it's a pain in the neck. Talk—on the phone, before, throughout, and after meetings, during Managing by Walking Around—is the wind that keeps the ship in motion. Most of it is boring beyond the capacity of the human spirit to comprehend. Key conversations, however, happen with regularity if you're on a roll, and you've got to spot them, and make them happen. A conversation is key when it provides you with an opportunity to:

1. Get an assignment you want.
2. Build an alliance.
3. Schmooze with your betters.

First learn to comfortably break the ice, which can be thick
with years of rime. Start with eye contact. "Forbisher! Hi! How
go the financials on the Ottowa project?" is a superb next step,
if you can't think of anything more personal. If Forbisher does
not seem inclined to conversation, move on through with an air
of efficient preoccupation.

Remember that people who do a lot of listening are generally considered great conversationalists. And don't mistake
chattiness with gossip, which has its place, and its pleasures.

Corporate Communications, see Public Relations.

Corporate Culture was first discovered in large, com-
plex organizations like the postal service and General Motors.
Enthused anthropologists subsequently found it lurking in
business structures large and small, and now no corporation
can be without one. A company's culture is, in fact, nothing
more than the experience of working there. When analyzing
your own culture, and securing your position in it, look at a
variety of factors. These include: costume; working hours;
requisite jargon; attitudes toward profanity and humor; the
relative importance of telephone, in-person and paper communications; attitudes toward alcohol and drugs; and many,
many others. Some standards, probably the more superficial,
you'll want to conform to rigidly. Others you'll have to keep at
bay because they do damage to your dignity or poker time. If
you're happy, liked by a moderate number of people, and, most
of all, busy with a range of interesting projects, you've probably got the culture in your bones, so forget about it and do
what comes naturally. Self-confidence is welcome anywhere.

Corporate Tree is the vertical reporting structure that
makes a business work. Like a tree, it is thickest at its base,
reaching upward in ever-narrowing tendrils until it culminates
at the juicy flowers way up top. No part of the trunk, no single
branch is dispensable, and decay of any one level endangers the
life of the entire organism. The following hierarchy is typical, if
not absolute:

• *Submanagement* toils at the phone, the word processor, the open cubicle. Sometimes they are actors, abstract expressionists, opera singers—dreamers who remain happy and apart. Others are professionals, fiercely proud of the hold they have on the men and women they serve. They do not make policy, and they do not make money. If you are now in a submanagement function, and sincerely feel you have the ability and desire to move into the passing lane, press hard on your boss to let you prove yourself with new kinds of work and more responsibility. Then bust your hump to make the break from the amateurs to the minor leagues.

• *Manager* status, in some organizations, means tremendous responsibility and a gaggle of underlings. In others, it means a pile of work, no recognition, and a salary that is depressing, if not shocking, after taxes. But you've got a leg up. Don't stop now.

• *Directors* are created to breathe heavily down the necks of the vice-presidents above them. They seldom, however, break into the club from within the same corporation, since no top executive likes to see young and talented sprouts knocking off their mentors. To reach senior management with all its perks and aggravations, you may have to make the quantum leap to another corporate tree.

• *Vice-Presidents* under fifty are what being in business is all about. Vital, powerful, immersed in the conceptual problems of an intricate business, making good money, bonuses, and with the chance to get away from home at will and visit strange locations in outlying areas, abuse company plastic, and, most of all, tell a variety of people what to do pretty much at will—it's nice work if you can get it.

And you can get it if you try. Most everyone can become a vice-president somewhere. In fact, you should expect to, and not settle for less. When you feel you're ready, look within your company and see, honestly, if there is a spot for you in a year or so. If not, start looking elsewhere and be patient. VP posts don't grow on corporate trees.

• *Senior Vice-President:* Who knows what it is. It's either a man who never will be king or an heir apparent. Try to tell the difference. The old geezer you ignore in the hallway today could be King Tut tomorrow.

• *President* is the first level of "key" or "top" management. With presidency comes tremendous authority, responsibility, and stock options, not to mention cash. Unfortunately, you can't spend it. You're too busy living off the company's dough at mandatory late-night dinners with the controller and motivational breakfasts with the marketing crew. Your time belongs to the corporation. Your mind, too, as well as your heart. You are, in fact, *it*. And there is no climbing down from your perch—only jumping off. Fortunately, there are parachutes designed to protect you from just such an eventuality.

• *Chief Operating Officer* is often the president, too. He's the guy in charge of implementing plans, not necessarily making them, and a soldier is only as good as his orders. So, if he's smart, he defers to a higher power just like everyone else, unless, of course, he's a flaming entrepreneur, or an egomaniac who overestimates his own value and worth. At his height, it's easy for him to forget he's replaceable. But he is. Just like you.

• *Chief Executive Officer* is the most important brain in the outfit. He must have command of the corporate gestalt in all its wonderful and terrifying complexity, managing people, resources, and projects—above all making money. Like priests or actors, chief executives totally cede their lives to their work. They do it not for money, which they give to their nominal families, but for love: of power, of achievement, of combat. Just look in the eye of any retired CEO and you'll see how happy a new Rolls makes you when the deli is the only place you have to go.

• *Chairman* is often the CEO. When he's not, he's probably there because he founded the place and cannot be ousted, or, perhaps, to make speeches. Sort of like Queen Elizabeth—the highest title, the greatest pomp, the smallest power. When, however, the chairman is the CEO, it may be useful to remember what a six-hundred-and-fifty-pound gorilla eats for breakfast. (Whatever he wants. Maybe even you.)

Corporation is an association of individuals, created under law, having a function and continuous existence independent of any single member. If that sounds like a government, it's no accident. That's what a corporation is, with its own regulations, power structure, defenses, and mythology. Some are international totalitarian machines, with tiers of fearful cadres from Madras to Toledo reporting to ever more calcified strata of committees and offices, all under the baleful or benign eye of a Big Brother in Houston, Detroit, or New York. Others are feudal states, in which serfs slave for lords, who fight for barons, who labor for princes, who live and die for the king. Still others are mellow communes, where the larger good of the collective dictates high standards of selflessness, mutual sacrifice, and shared effort.

No matter the culture, the first principle of any corporation is to perpetuate itself, and to grow. Help it do that, obey its stated and unspoken bylaws, and you will thrive. As in any government, good political skills are more than invaluable: they spell survival. Don't worry if business-as-usual has a slightly Machiavellian aftertaste. Politics may make strange bedfellows, but it sure beats the hell out of sleeping alone.

Correspondence, like shaving, should be done first thing in the morning, when the mind is unprepared for more serious work but ready to grapple with superficial necessities. Dictate if you can, but be careful to edit your output once it's on paper; it's going to be terrible. If your utterances make irretrievably bad copy, peck out your chores on your own if you want to. Whatever you do, don't let it slide. Don't forget to throw away all useless letters unanswered. Marginal in-box material should be handled by phone. Everyone admires a guy who travels light.

Cost Center is part of the organization that produces nothing but work. It generally sows not, neither does it reap. But that doesn't mean it's not important. When it carries out its assigned function, a cost center—strategic planning, accounting, public relations, human resources (or, for those who speak English, personnel) all the way up to the uttermost and costliest tippytop of senior management itself—supports the segments of the corporate body that keep the shekels coming in.

No animal can hunt on sheer instinct. Eyes, ears and a passable brain are also a necessity. For further discussion, see **Profit Center.**

Cost Cutter, in some cases, is nothing more than a bean-counter with a necessary job to do. Corporations, like bourgeoisie, tend to gain weight with each passing year, stretching a little more about the middle out of sheer indolence and not really worrying about it. After a time, though, expenses mount, margins dip, and the fat begins to slow the organism down. Enter the cost cutter, who may find a load of things from paper clips to long-distance calls to ream out of everyone's hide. That's okay. Cutting out an executive's first-class travel perks is better than cutting his throat.

Sometimes, however, cost cutters are called in expressly to organize and administer mass executions. These individuals are the lowest form of corporate life. For further discussion, see **Hitman.**

Costume, see Style.

Creativity is one of the few big concepts that has not descended into jargon in the mouth of business, perhaps because, unlike *commitment* and *excellence,* it will never go out of style. Ideas in this world are always in short supply—even bad ones. People who can draw on their inner resources at will, and come up with thoughts others can, at least, discuss, are an asset to an organization that must constantly generate the illusion of planned activity. So do your best to tap your creativity when people are looking for solutions. And don't be afraid to put your ideas across, either, no matter how dumb you may suspect them to be. Creativity lies in the quantity of thought produced as well as the quality. If you hit one out of three, you'll still be carrying a major-league batting average.

Credenza is the thigh-level hutch in which files, reports and other office paraphernalia are housed and, when necessary, hidden. It is a conceptual object that does not exist outside the contemporary workplace, a totem of executive status and pretension. Your credenza, if you achieve one, will be as organized as the inside of your brain. Good luck.

Cretins wouldn't recognize a good idea if it came up and bit them. They are thick, and clot agendas. Cretinous behavior is not limited to the stupid, unfortunately. It also afflicts the proud. A powerful cretin must be handled very carefully, with excruciating politeness, his criticisms, no matter how appallingly dim-witted, entertained. He'll appreciate the effort and may just back your project, even though he still doesn't get it.

Crisis is obvious. When the CEO calls on Friday at four P.M. and wants to know where the third-quarter financials for the northeast district are and you haven't started them because you thought someone else was doing it, that's a crisis. When a protégé is indicted for indecent exposure at the company picnic leaving his family and a two-million-dollar budget line in ruins, that's one, too. The internal signs of crisis are unmistakable: a nauseating vacuum in the pit of your gut, a black vortex swimming before your eyes, all the classic symptoms of terror. After the initial jolt, pull yourself together and actively manage the situation lest it do the same to you. Contact your boss immediately and brief him. Let him know that you are in control, even if you're not. Then get together with some folks you trust, work up a strategy, and implement it, even if it takes all night. Be thankful it's a crisis, not a major fuck-up.

Crunch is the result of bad time management. You've promised too much to too many people, jerked around instead of hunkering down, the deadlines are upon you, and now you have to pay. Tough. Taxi drivers stay behind the wheel for twenty-four hours at a stretch during Christmastime. Farmers rise at five A.M. to milk cows. Why should you be immune from hard labor? Roll up your sleeves and get to work.

Customer, as in *The Customer,* is the most important concept in warm and toasty, excellence-based mythologies. Business units need a raison d'être just as much as anyone. Some choose *winning,* others *quality,* but when a company is involved in selling a product or service directly to the Great Unwashed—cars, airline tickets, amusement worlds—they often find it necessary to glorify The Customer to their own troops. That's because the actual customer is often an ill-tempered, irrational, puling complainer with whom you cannot argue and win, not if you want to keep his money coming. In the best service organizations, traditional Judeo-Christian religion is replaced by an almost Schweitzerian reverence for the John and Jane Does out there who are paying the bills with their cash. If you're caught up in such an organization, repress the urge to sneer. It could be bad for your health.

Cutbacks mean loss of life, no matter what you hear from optimists around you. The word is one of the comfortable euphemisms used by management to announce layoffs, wholesale retirements, and mass executions. Develop sensitive antennae and listen for the distant whisper of any trouble. If you hear that cutbacks (or a *reorganization*) are in the offing, start working to save your life. Do everything you can—through work and friendship—to make yourself indispensable to those who are sharpening the cleavers. It doesn't hurt to put out a few feelers elsewhere, either. If you should make it through unscathed, or improve your position in the new, leaner organization, try not to indulge in too much survivor guilt. The business belongs to the living.

D

Decentralization is the corporate excuse for firing head-quarters personnel and thinning out the head count. For example: a company has been holding down the national accounting function in Dallas with a team of fifteen highly qualified, experienced personnel. One day, after much self-examination and waves of apocalyptic rumor, the ax falls. Two headquarters accountants are retained, left to slave over the former duties of the multitudes; six are immediately laid off, with apologies. The final six are offered splendid posts in the decentralized structure. Unfortunately for them, these generous opportunities are located in Salt Lake City, Walla Walla, Petaluma, Ft. Myers, Toledo, and Scranton. All decline, and local people are hired at lower salaries to fill the new regional positions. Net effect: head count down by six, pay levels down by 340 percent. The impression of fiscal control has been created.

Decentralized management is designed to make a national operation more responsive to its customers, placing decision-making one step closer to the point of purchase. It can be very good medicine for bloated behemoths, especially in customer service operations. It still stinks for those who are to be decentralized, so the slightest whiff of it should put you on yellow alert if you work in a headquarters operation. It means nothing more or less than the destruction of your function. To fight it out and survive, you've got to convince the hierarchy that a national oversight of your function is necessary to the bottom line. The role of central headquarters, if they ask, is to provide themes and standards, keep score on the field offices, and maintain honesty and accountability nationwide. In short, you are the heart of the culture. Every watch needs a mainspring. Your survival—and that of the company—depends on your ability to sell that point.

Delegating is the ability to change personal labor into management of others. Great delegators view every task as one that rightfully belongs to someone else. After the task is passed along formally, the delegator then keeps an eye on the project so that later he can claim a hand in its success. Develop this art and you, too, will be targeted as talented management. For the higher the manager, the less actual, hands-on grunt work he or she is expected to do, leaving top management free to do what it does best, which is, presumably, to manage. Delegation is broken down into four discrete phases:

• *Evaluation:* In which the job is received and analyzed, and the determination made that it need not be done personally.

• *Assignment:* In which the hapless subordinate is targeted, evaluated, and informed of the good news.

• *Supervision:* In which ongoing pressure is placed on the subordinate, your guidance offered, and their progress charted. Central to this phase is delivery of the product to your desk with plenty of time for your review. Remember that the finished object must come from you, the delegator, since it was to your office that the request originally came.

• *Reflected Glory:* In which your subordinate is accorded all due kudos, and you receive points for having managed the project to a successful completion.

When you stop sweating and start delegating, you're on your way into the manager's club. So get rolling today and have someone else handle whatever it is immediately. Then do lunch.

Desk is you. Cherish it, and let it be just that. Got a toy train you like? A rubber duckie? Bring it in and plump it proudly on your blotter. It will be good for three months of premeeting yuks. Trophies—any kind—are excellent, too, for obvious reasons. Don't be obsessive about keeping your desk neat, either, unless that's the way you work. Clutter does not automatically spell disorder, and military organization can signal a bored and boring mind. A man whose desk is clear at three P.M. may be simply getting set for quitting time two hours early. So allow your desk to display all the energy, creativity, confusion, all the terror and grandeur of your life there. If the culture starts to lean on you with "clean desk" standards, clearly express your opposition to the statute and keep a sharp lookout for the corporate police. Word usually precedes their coming. And if, finally, they won't let you run your own desk, dump your stuff on the floor and work from there.

It's a good idea, though, to create at least the impression of order for yourself at the end of the day. That way you can start the new morning by maintaining the illusion of control for a couple of hours. For the tool that hides a multitude of sins, see **In-Box.**

Dinner Parties with associates are an opportunity for gregarious types, but for the shy they can be a torment of inadequacy and shame. If you're something of a social cripple at formal gatherings where small talk, nose to nose with acquaintances who are not friends, is mandatory, it's important to realize that most people share your plight. The ability to yammer about superficialities is a gift. Some got it and some ain't.

That doesn't mean you have to spend the evening shrinking into yourself like a slug on salt. Figure out who else is languishing behind the great wall of silence and strike up the halting beginnings of a queer conversation. If you're not embarrassed by pauses, he won't be either. Actual words passing between you is better, though. Keep in mind that when you ask an average person about himself, he has something to say for two minutes, egomaniacs somewhat longer. As he either rhapsodizes buckets, or ekes out a puny something about his life, take the opportunity to nod, say uh-huh, and offer a few comments about you. Field a solid quip if you've got one. Don't push, but don't be a dead fish—it's a dinner party, remember? Talk about the weather, real estate, whatever. Then say you have to get a drink. There. Was that so bad? It's called chat, and after you master the rudiments, when the fear of the void isn't fusing your lips, you may move on to subjects with some content. Movies, sports, and when you're a master, industry gossip and, finally, rumor. Who knows to what career heights and depths such practiced schpritzing may lead?

Divestiture is the surgical removal (by sale) of an unwanted corpuscle from the corporate body. When someone else is divested, it usually seems to make good business sense to everyone. When it's you, on the other hand, you'll find yourself railing against the cold and omnivorous heart of the business beast. There is, however, no point in spitting up all over yourself when divestiture is performed on you. Just slam out a state-of-the-art résumé on the best word processor available. Then hit the street, discreetly. Look at it this way: you probably won't find anything, but think how crazy you'd be going if you weren't looking. In the meantime, get set to jump through hoops—it's time to prove your worth to the new bottom line. For a discussion, see **Mergers.**

Dog and Pony Show is a very special kind of presentation, one in which style is every bit as important as substance. Actually, it's more important, since people won't hear what you're saying unless they see charts, slides, and maybe even a multimedia presentation with the schmaltziest score since Bruckner. Got the annual budget forecast to present to the parent corporation in six weeks? It's showtime, ladies and gentlemen. In some wise cultures, the basic dog-and-pony is delivered with nothing more than overhead transparencies and index cards. Discussion is encouraged, and the mood is sedate. Elsewhere, it may be necessary to call in a design firm and a computer-generated slide house, and to pass your formal copy through clearance loops worthy of Dante. Whatever the maximum requirement, that's the one you want to deliver. But don't be stuffy. It's a dog-and-pony. Speak loud, have fun, and don't bump into the furniture.

Doodling is one form of cogitation, and some of the deepest thinkers are the most active doodlers. So don't think that because someone is doodling, he isn't 100 percent tuned-in. He may be listening with an inner ear. If his mouth is still working while he's sketching doggies, boats, and curlicues, don't sweat it. He's hanging in there.

Doodling is also one of the best means of staying awake at a meeting one considers useless. If a guy begins doodling at the outset of your meeting and doesn't come up for air until the first coffee break, it's a bad sign. It kind of conveys that he's not interested.

If you're a notepad graffiti artist, enjoy yourself. But make sure you don't unconsciously scribble out something you'd rather not reveal. Idly inking a skull and crossbones while meeting with the vice-president of corporate security isn't exactly good politics. Stick to trees and duckies.

Door is your portal to freedom. Behind a closed door, you can think, write, dream, call your wife to apologize, hang upside down with your feet on your desk, and stare off into space like a sloth. You can also take a private meeting on your home turf, leverage that can in no way be established without a door. A man without a door is a slave. Watch office space in your department like a hawk and agitate for a door. Title and money are sure to follow. Guys with doors are on the permanent squad, and without one you might as well, in a profound sense, be a secretary.

Under no circumstances, however, should you abuse your door. A persistently closed door generates a bad stench down the entire corridor. It's a slap in the face to the collective energy of the operation, and often a signal flare sent up by a sinking ship. So keep it open until you want to be alone. Then exercise your executive priority and bask in silence and privacy. It's as necessary to your success as heavy lunching. Solitary reflection will always be important in an enterprise with problems to solve.

Downside is all the bad things that could result from a specific action. As in: "Before we bless that plan we'll have to consider the downside implications." Or: "The downside, Jack, is that we're transferring you to Brazil." It's a good idea to spend some time looking at the downside of every situation, lest it become more than mere speculation. On the other hand, every downside supports its opposite. For a discussion, see **Upside.**

Drinks is one of the most venerated institutions in business life, the glue that bonds gray multinational droids to slick sharks in Hawaiian shirts. Drinks are the opportunity to hear the worst jokes in human history, to share stories about vendors and competitors, to enjoy a moment of comradeship with men you will never really know, and, best of all, to get politely drunk. Consistently sharing drinks with the same crowd can also lead to the rare jewel of friendship. It's not the only way, but it's not the worst, either.

Fortunately, most industries have a wild variety of excuses for drinking together, from the random whim of two chummy executives to the mass drunking of seven hundred middle managers. And where liquor flows, there is no fear, no danger, and no agenda.

Ah, there's the rub. It's quite possible that, when drinking with corporate pros, where the bourbon is free, the chicken wings are hot, and the female vice-presidents have their ties off, you may say something stupid or barf without thinking upon the chairman's tie. It is therefore best to appoint someone your guardian at social functions when you know you're going to get drunk. And drink with your head, not over it.

Each meal has its beverage protocol. The three questions are *whether, when,* and *how much:*

Breakfast

Whether: Not alone.

When: As soon as the highest-ranking person at the table does, but only if you wish. Nobody blames a guy for not getting loaded first thing in the morning.

How much: One, and keep it to a Bloody Mary, Screwdriver, or Mimosa, something tasteful and discreet. A breakfast of dry toast with a belt of bourbon on the side sends an unmistakable message about you.

Lunch

Whether: When in Rome.

When: Immediately, but again, try not to be the first to order. It's no fun to call for a double only to hear the seven other lunchers at your table order Perrier with lime.

How much: One distilled spirit, one beer or wine with the meal, and maybe a brandy after if the other guy is amicable. Unless lunching is your occupation, you may have to do something businesslike sometime before five. Strolling into a key meeting reeking of Velamints, all rosy, jaunty, and jolly from good fellowship and wassail, is suicidal. Come back from lunch prepared for anything. Control before five o'clock is the name of the game.

Dinner

Whether: Yes. You're on your own time now.

When: When the waiter arrives.

How much: Stay just a nose behind the pack. You may just generate a reputation for sobriety and self-control you do not deserve.

After Dinner

Whether: Sure!

When: Since you started at dinner, what's the difference?

How much: Don't do anything you can't live down. Remember, this isn't really the fun factory, no matter how much jocularity is zinging through the air. Taking a leak in the street while the chief financial officer looks on may be unwise, unless he's a remarkably fine man indeed.

Finally, strange as it may seem, there are places where people are encouraged to drink lightly, less, or not at all. If you labor in such a gulag, you'll have to get bent on your own time. Do not fail to do so. Excess in the pursuit of liberty is no vice.

Drugs are illegal, unhealthy, and, worse, out of style. The ideal of the decade is the Healthy Man, free of all excesses except, perhaps, a passion for rigorous exercise and spending money. Avowed enjoyment of controlled substances definitely marks you as a relic of a golden, fuzzy, bygone age. The man of the eighties gets high on deal making, not 'ludes. And elderly strategic planners in deep gray don't like hippies and lawbreakers much, either. You don't want to come in every morning with a runny nose, snuffling and wheezing like a warthog. A man could get put in prison, even fired. Business is straight, and don't you forget it.

In some industries that shall remain nameless, on the other hand, the coke spoon has replaced the swizzle stick and designer drugs abound. Even in such rarefied locations, though, it's wise to keep a low profile when engaging in any of those activities that reveal your true tastes and proclivities. What the organization doesn't know won't hurt you.

E

Eating well is the best revenge, especially when it's free. It is also a time to think, relax, and remember you are a person with hungers that transcend the office and its demands. Unfortunately, in the present business atmosphere, where Eisenhoweresque go-getterism is the unquestioned ethos, the sacred meal hours have been totally invaded by venal and insecure operators who feel every waking minute should be assigned a goal, a strategy, a purpose. The first purpose of any meal is the ingestion of food. Don't forget that, and don't listen to anyone who tells you differently. Meals are one of the last rituals in contemporary life. Eat with whomever you please, and don't get hung in the round of fruitless munching and gabbing that passes for current business eating. If people adhered to the old rule, and never talked while their mouths were full, the world would be a better place, and a lot more work would get done, too.

There are only three acceptable forms of fueling up on company time:

• *Eating with Friends:* Not optional—mandatory. A two-hour lunch with a compatriot, trading company scuttlebutt, can be terrific therapy between salary reviews. Don't go hog-wild on the decor and price tab, though, if it's just a pal you're with. Save the elegance for strangers.

51

• *Eating for a Good Business Reason:* There's a certain amount of professional tap-dancing going on, but selling and digesting don't always mix. So keep things lite, and have stuff to talk about in the interstitial phases. Like the wine list. Opulence to the limits of corporate largess should attend serious work. You are out there pitching at a time in which you could be thinking, relaxing, or taking a break from other people in your face. That deserves a reward. Try the prime rib.

• *Meals at your desk:* A solitary tuna on toast can be a lot more soothing than a four-course force-feeding at La Côte Basque. A meal at your desk will give you a little of the perspective that comes from solitude, a momentary recollection of the You that exists outside the job. Don't worry about missing all that yak. Haven't you had enough fatuous meetings today?

When eating with others, by the way, keep in mind that in most civilized nations, eating a foodstuff of your choice is acceptable behavior at meals. It's unnecessary to make believe you're Scarlett O'Hara at the cotillion and eat nothing but lint and water because you want to send a power message, or stuff yourself with raw meat when you feel like a chef salad because you're trying to outmacho some heavyweight.

There's been a lot of trendy quasi-wisdom written about seating and food selection at meals—what to eat, what not, where to sit, where not. Meals should be an expression of self and an opportunity for spontaneity and enjoyment. Eating for power, not joy, is an admission that, for you to succeed, every single situation, no matter how potentially benign, must be manipulated, controlled. That's essentially timid, and damn nerdy, too.

Eating with another guy is, finally, a good way to tell if he can be trusted. The face beaming across the table at you with tomato sauce on its chin generally isn't going to spit in your eye fifteen minutes later at the quarterly budget review.

Eccentricity is any expression of personality that reveals a glimpse of the man you are behind your corporate veil. In some corporate environments this may mean ordering Dover sole instead of slabs of beef at lunch. In any highly structured society, all strong men are, in a deep sense, eccentric since their individual traits, the habits and tastes that they cannot help but show—in short, their humanity—mark them as something both less and more than the rigid mean decreed by the culture. Men who are worried about their eccentricities are doomed to fail. It is encouraging to note that the higher the executive, the more weird his behavior, perhaps because power breeds privilege. The successful player expresses his entire personality in his work, which in itself renders him automatically eccentric. So don't worry about your oddities. They may be a mark of greatness. Of course, that doesn't mean you can bring your Walkman to a board meeting and listen to your Motown tapes while the financial report is being delivered. Eccentricity is tolerated in organizations that value creativity. Insanity is frowned upon almost everywhere.

Elevators are tiny rooms where conversation, circumscribed by the proximity of your destination, is impossible. Everything but Muzak is trivial in an elevator. If there's heavy interoffice traffic in your elevator, and you often find yourself standing next to heavyweights on the way to somewhere, try to bring some reading material with you. Memos, reports, letters, whatever, as long as it can distract you. You may as well create the illusion that you are on your way to something crucial and cannot be bothered with anything but minimal, friendly greetings. And don't be afraid of dead silence, either. It's better than blurting out something dense in a paroxysm of anxious, inappropriate verbosity. If, however, you are light of tongue and capable of generating a brief one-liner, don't be bashful. The man who can leave a crowd of people chuckling after only three floors is destined to be included in many longer, more substantial meetings.

Enemies are the product of success. The bland have none. That doesn't mean that it's advisable to collect them. Whether an enemy is powerful, wise, stupid, venal, or misguided, he can torpedo you at any time, and will, probably when you least

expect it. As long as he's viable, i.e., has at least one friend in
senior management, an enemy is a time bomb waiting to go off
in your face. And even if his beef with you is totally off the wall,
it's still evidence of defeat that you allowed things to come to
this sorry pass. If you can't eliminate an enemy by guile or
muscle, try cordiality, and a little discreet support of his objectives. It's amazing how fast an enemy turns into a colleague
after you cast a vote for one of his budget lines.

If, of course, you disagree with his notion to administer
urine tests to all employees biweekly, then settle in for a battle
you cannot lose. Fight the contest on the merits of the issue, by
the way. Letting things get personal is an indication that you're
locked in a death grip with your enemy, a sight most people find
repugnant. Remember that a policy of live-and-let-live, while
easy with friends, is most important with guys who hate you.
Once he understands you're willing to cultivate a slow and
enduring hatred, rather than push for imminent resolution, he
may be content to remain a thorn in your side rather than a
knife in your heart.

Entertaining should be done in the office and its en-
virons, unless you live at Versailles and your spouse is socially
gifted. It need not be done over drinks and petit-fours, either. If
you've got the touch, you can entertain anywhere.

• *Entertaining Others:* This may be done with either money
or charm. Charm costs less, but is riskier. Still, if you can drop
by the vice-president of marketing's lair, lob a few con-
versational gems aloft, and leave him feeling expansive and
brave, that's a real asset. The same thing can be said of open
meetings. The man who can keep things entertaining in the
midst of discussions on the dissolution of the Farm Products
Division is a prime resource to an organization intent on excis-
ing its navel.

There are times, of course, when you want to show a guy a
good time. It could be a boss, whose firm command over you is
blossoming into friendship. Or a client, who's already sold but
wants the last little stroke for good measure. Or the direct-sales
team that's had a terrific third quarter and is in need of recogni-

tion. You want to get close, enjoy yourself away from the clank and rattle of business-as-usual. Fine. Does that mean they have to come home with you? Not unless you want them to. Rule of thumb: if you feel you'll have to apologize for your wife or husband, or the paint job, or the mold in your refrigerator, forget about it. If God had meant all of us to have their bosses and clients over to dinner in full view of their dogs and goldfish, He wouldn't have invented the overpriced restaurant.

    • *Entertaining Yourself:* This is most important. A bureaucracy is, by nature, a stultifying place, even when the pace is frenetic. It's always going on about something—a project, whim, fire drill, showdown, etc. After a while, the constant grind and whirr of perpetual motion in no discernible direction can become as boring as paralysis. Keeping yourself entertained is the only way to take the sting out of the pervading sense that activity is taking place simply for its own sake.

    Lunching with friends and interesting strangers is a start, shooting a deep and satisfying hole in the middle of the day, but it's a bad habit if you've got an actual job to do that doesn't involve interpersonal relations at their utmost. Whistling the tunes of your generation works, too, as do periodic and refreshing calls to friends within your network, or from your past. Whether you take a walk in the park, buy some cigars, or close your door and read the paper (a necessary task for every manager, isn't it?), by all means keep things entertaining for yourself. If you don't, you won't be many laughs for others, now, will you? Perhaps the most entertaining thing of all, of course, is interesting work. Landing the choice assignments is the key. For a discussion, see **Gigs.**

Entrepreneurial Spirit is the ability to go it alone on the strength of a good idea. Not all people have it. In fact, a lot of the best business minds are about as adventurous as Marcel Proust. Those who enjoy an entrepreneurial bent are cursed, however, as well as fortunate. Theirs is the lot to build a company into greatness, only to have the organizational type take over and send him out to pasture at the ripe age of thirty-five.

    While it lasts, however, the entrepreneurial phase of an

operation is heady stuff. New ideas are being generated at a whirlwind pace, new products being fielded, new life being spawned and money coined—all flowing from the freewheeling style of the liberated mentality that runs the joint. If you're able to dream up schemes that work and sell your ideas to others, more power to you. Drive your talent into the ground and don't let the small minds tell you what cannot be done. American history is studded with stories of entrepreneurs who started with a pile of dirt and lived to endow universities. The key time in any entrepreneurial effort is when success is at hand. That's when the need for organization, for a machine to perpetuate the original solutions, becomes critical. The entrepreneur who can negotiate that hurdle and build a loyal structure around his bones can follow in the footsteps of Henry Ford, Thomas Alva Edison, and Ted Turner.

Ethics are the body of moral principles that govern a culture, whether it likes it or not. Whatever its particulars within your company, an ethical system means little if it is not expressed in day-to-day action, in the fabric of your dealings with people. Most organizations, excepting government, have a rather strict ethical system, at least on record. This ethos usually involves such things as honor, loyalty, honesty, and courtesy, among other attributes. An accompanying unspoken ethos, however, usually gives you some latitude if you're dealing with a jerk whose stupidity is killing an important deal. Remember: The overriding ethic in most business societies is *success*.

The only real ethical system—that which must supersede all others—is, of course, your own. If you're not aware you have one, don't worry. Maybe it's simple and inarticulate, and so much a part of you it has never been questioned. Unless you're a good German in the worst sense, ethics are there: the little siren that goes off inside you when a smarmy proposal bursts into the air, the inability to go along with an unscrupulous program even if it would make the company some money. That, by the way, is when ethical behavior counts—when it hurts. For an ethic is not an attitude. It's a set of rules you do not break. And it can't survive without your backbone behind it. Yes, this is easier said than done when the ethical system of your company, or lack of one, conflicts with your own sense of what is right and wrong. Remember that an expression of moral judgment need not be noisy, and need not destroy you, to be effective in making its point and perpetuating your belief in your own dignity, such as it is. The only audience you're playing to is yourself. Satisfy that, and you cannot then be false to any man. Unless you work for Beechnut, in which case you'll just have to quit.

Excellence, currently a mega-buzzword, may be obsolete by the time you read this, replaced with something more immediately concrete to business minds at the moment—like Greatness, or Integrity, or Service. It doesn't matter. These trendoid terms burst onto the business scene periodically, and they are interchangeable. They appear to hold rock-hard, eternal truths in their cores, but in fact they are hollow, because whatever the heavy concept of the hour may be, no matter how popular and resonant within your culture, it doesn't change the basic nature of your relationship to your work, or to your employer, one whit. No matter how great your commitment to excellence, if they suddenly stopped paying you, you'd go home.

All honest men try to do the best job they can, and to preserve, in the face of all evidence to the contrary, their sense of the uniqueness and grandeur of their lives. They don't need business writers to define, appropriate, and mechanize what is best about their work. Besides, excellence, if it exists as anything outside of business language, is a process, not a pound of chopped liver. You can't make it by reading the recipe, and you can't run out and buy it. Work your eight hours and do the best job you can every day. That should be Excellence enough for any organization.

Executives are men who have worked long enough to have attained the privilege of telling other people what to do. The higher the executive, the more people he can boss around. Top executives give entire organizations marching orders. But all executives have masters, even the sleek serge suits at the top.

And all are vulnerable, and, therefore, human. Lose any intimidation you may feel about the executive strata around and above you. They're just a bunch of guys trying to stay afloat, and they could probably use your help. Never, however, lose your ability to show respect for them. After working twenty years in the business, a superior executive may feel he's earned that. You will feel the same, when you get there.

Expense Accounts must be handled with honesty and discretion, and abused within those boundaries. A serious executive is expected to rack up expenses worthy of his power and stature within the organization, so if it's even halfway reasonable, go for it, especially if your salary isn't all you think it could be.

The challenge is to maintain a coherent *level of rational abuse,* including all items that could conceivably be explained, if you had to. Company auditors are like the IRS. They don't care a whole lot what you do, as long as it's relatively consistent. When you suddenly put through a radical upward bump, however, their computers will spit you out for a second look. So give yourself every benefit of the doubt, and keep your expenditures at an appropriate level to your rank.

An expense account not exploited ultimately dies of neglect—use it or lose it.

F

Facial Hair is your own business once it's in full flower. In excess, or in transition, it's a public problem. Only truly nerdish organizations will bother you about an existing beard or mustache as long as the offending luxuriance is trimmed to a sane level. A barbe the size of a mushmelon, however, doesn't inspire a whole lot of confidence in dour financial types looking for sober analyses, and for obvious reasons you don't want to go around looking like an anarchist. But tasteful facial hair seems to be one of the only permanent concessions won from authority in the 1960s, so wear a tidy 'stache, if it makes you look keen, or, if you must, a beard that hugs your face like a slipcover.

But don't grow it on company time. No one looks good with a grotty slime of fuzz on his face, and an obvious growth campaign alerts people that a part of you doesn't really give a damn how you look. That's a complicated message to send to conformists. So, if you want to conceal your trembling upper lip or mudslide chin, or simply feel like hiding behind your manhood for a while, take your three weeks together this year and come back hairy. Then be prepared for people to treat you like a stranger. After all, you are. Business relations are heavily grounded in appearances. And that pink and smiling face of yours may come across differently when all that shows are your eyes and teeth.

Finally, whatever you do, don't grow a beard without a mustache, unless you are Amish. And sideburns went out with John Sebastian. Nonconformity is one thing, buffoonery is quite another.

Faking It is a bad idea, unless you do it well. Fortunately, the fear of God can make a straightforward dullard incandescent on subjects he knows nothing about. In any case, don't overdo it. An honest expression of ignorance on a complex subject is often welcomed. It gives the reigning expert a chance to school you, an opportunity that most accomplished and egotistical pundits relish when they're not too busy. Occasionally, however, you may find yourself woefully uninformed on an issue that requires your understanding and attention. That's a bad fact to make public. Faking it may also be required when a meeting enters subjects you need to know nothing about and would just as soon sleep through.

Nodding, augmented with a well-placed "uh-huh," is the time-honored way to begin. It was good enough for Freud, so why not you? The technique soothes people and lets them know you're paying attention. It's also noncommittal, which is good, because you have no idea what they're talking about. In one-on-one conversations, rampant agreement is effective, tinged with a shade of intelligent skepticism, as in, "Terrific idea, Ron. Outstanding. I think I'd have to see some paper on it before I really grasped all its implications, though." In open meetings, where you can almost doze and not get caught, it may be wise to interject an occasional comment to show you're in the same room. "We've been studying that, but I don't know what to think yet," is an acceptable response to, "What do you think about the viability of digital circuitry in the modal units?" Finally, remember that dumb silence may be easily mistaken for intelligent disapproval. It's far, far better to keep your mouth shut than reveal the vast chasm that lies beyond your vacant smile.

Favors are kindnesses done out of good will, rather than duty, or, in their purest form, the expectation of future remuneration. They should be given freely or not at all, but sometimes you will have to comply with an unreasonable request. The boss who asks you to stay late to rework his wife's résumé, for instance, is not asking for a legitimate favor—he's leaning on you, pure and simple. The colleague who begs you to cover his ass while he's at the ballgame may do the same for you one day. And while that's not remuneration, exactly, it just might come in handy on a summer afternoon you'd rather spend in your garden. So lade out favors when the spirit moves you, and occasionally when it doesn't.

Keep tabs on both the bogus ones you've done under compulsion and the fine, upstanding variety you've performed for friends. One day, maybe soon, you'll want to call in those chips. At salary review time, for example, or when you have to arrange a delicate meeting and need some help, or, perhaps, when you find out the big industry gathering is to be held in Rio this year and need a reason to attend. Pick your time, then ask for a little quid pro quo. Isn't it about time your selfless generosity paid off?

Feminism has permeated business life to varying degrees, its effects most profound—as in society at large—in the upper echelons where women have a greater education and sense of their own power and worth. In that stratum, the doctrine has achieved its objectives only too well, creating a class of female managers who, at their worst, are just as opinionated, judgmental, and manipulative as their male counterparts. At the same time, the success of uncommon women has done little to improve the lot of the garden variety, and sisterhood is invisible in most corporate settings. If anything, female managers tend to be less tender toward members of their gender, perhaps believing that displays of feminist indulgence would mark them as different (and therefore inferior) to the men around them who are under no such constraint. Equality has come to equal conformity with a vengeance.

We now live in a business world with many women who dress for success in severe pinstripe, white shirt, and tie, who talk like male stereotypes complete with profanity and butch machoisms, and who push their subordinates unmercifully, frowning on the poor droid who wants to get home at a less-than-workaholic hour to tend to his or her family.

On the other hand, the presence of accomplished women has feminized a good many male dinosaurs, who have come to respect women as equals and enjoy their company, opinions, and abilities. And in many places, the relationship between men and women is stabilizing, as teams with plenty of each get down to the real job at hand and forget about sexual politics. Everyone in business, male or female, high or low, must manage to a bottom line. That's a fact that makes sisters and brothers of us all.

Filing, to those not graced with anal-retentive personalities, is like going to the dentist. It's also a task amenable to infinite procrastination. Keep in mind that, while the prospect of a protracted session of filing may be enough to make you throw out your entire in-box in despair, in tiny doses it is tolerable, even purifying. So pick a day every couple of weeks, call your secretary in, and clear out the inner recesses of your pile. You'll feel a whole lot lighter after you do, and considerably more in control. Then go about collecting the detritus of your office with impunity until the purge is again due.

1. *Alphabetize:* And keep it that way. Once you start shoving things in at random, you're a dead man.

2. *Minimize:* Less is better. Couldn't you toss the drafts of your 1986 budget projections, now that the finished product is hanging around, bound and distributed, to haunt you?

3. *Partialize:* Try to break down subject matter into simple, diminutive parts. A file marked "Problem Areas" is of little use when you're trying to find the purchase order for that nuclear power plant the chairman forgot he ordered.

4. *Prioritize:* If you've got two filing cabinets (or, lucky you, a desk and a credenza), devote one to really important stuff and the other to material you have no immediate or foreseeable need for but are simply too paranoid to throw away.

5. *Scrutinize:* Scour your files periodically. Guys who move fast generally leave a lot behind.

Firing a person is a horrendous experience for you both, so once you have decided that termination is the only course, do it quickly and don't look back. There are few more sobering sights in corporate life than that of a future corpse wandering dazed in the wilderness, lonely, afraid, and too proud to ask for help. Allowing a marginally competent reportee to languish in limbo for a time is natural—maybe they'll shape up. But after a time, it's not kindness anymore, but cowardice. Think of it this way: you're keeping them from their next job, where they may be really happy.

Sometimes it may not be easy to get permission, however, to cleanse your reporting structure of a fuck-up, nincompoop, or weasel. Maybe they have seniority, or friends. It then becomes necessary to make a case that sticks. Break your strategy down into four phases:

1. *Documentation:* Keep all his screwy memos, festering as they are with rotten ideas and bad grammar. Take notes of your inane or infuriating conversations. In short, maintain a record of his malfeasance. When it's heavy with beef, proceed to step two.

2. *Warning:* Never fire somebody out of the blue—your move will almost always be overturned by cooler heads who care about procedure. Yes, you've got a right to execute the underlings of your choice, but they also have a right—the right to know why, and, perhaps, the right to change their ways. Don't worry. Odds are ninety to one they won't succeed.

3. *Clearance:* A courtesy call to human resources, or, if you think it politic, to your manager, is never out of line. If they respect your judgment, the road ahead will be clear. If they don't, it may be time to take another look at your judgment before others do.

4. *The Ax:* There is no right way to tell somebody they're out on the street, so forget about being elegant. If you've followed steps one through three, it's not going to come as any surprise to him. Give your reasons, brandish your documentation if you have to, and gently show the guy the door. It won't cost you anything to extol his talents a bit and blame the organization, either, if he's taking it badly. Your job is to fire him, not destroy him.

Friendship is necessary. Not only is life without it stale, flat and unprofitable, but friends also form the heart of your power base. So go the limit to develop those relationships that have promise, and be aware that they are only all the sweeter because they are doomed.

Business friendships generally thrive within that specific context and wither outside it. This does not invalidate them; in fact, all relationships need a framework to survive—a world of common heroes, villains, assumptions, and adventures. The intensity of business life also lends itself to the creation of fast and passionate affections. They are the one single aspect of your daily work that is unalterably and purely human—and they should be cherished for that. As time goes by, and old friends leave the infrastructure, or you do, you'll need to develop new allegiances and affections, as you have done before.

A solid friendship is as close to true love as you're going to get in the dry and flinty soil in which you work. So be loyal to your friends, whether they are power brokers or not. You will be repaid by the recognition that, after all, your life is not as alien to those childhood dreams as you thought.

G

Games are rife in organizations where there is some debate about the pecking order or a struggle over who is in control of a given situation. The resulting vacuum is a challenge to all those ambitious types who, by nature, abhor it, and seek to inhabit it. Interested players then line up to challenge one another's ability to perform on the turf in question. The games may be low-stakes tiddledywinks with nothing more on the line than reputation and bragging rights, or they may be life-and-death gladiatorial matches where enduring power is the prize and you've got to play to win, even if it means playing to hurt.

The trick is to identify the games you feel like taking part in and the ones you don't. There are some people who see all human interactions as one form of game or another. This worldview leads them to treat everything as a competition replete with rules, sides, winners, and losers. This is an effective motivator, for some. It's also a mighty narrow perspective, and guys obsessed with gamesmanship are often pathetically short on team spirit. Remember that you don't have to play if you don't want to. You can simply sit by the sidelines and keep score. Or you can kill the game altogether, if it gets dangerous, by calling an open meeting on the subject and turning it into work.

Gender is not an issue in a mature organization, although sex often is. Each individual is expected to perform a function, adhere to the cultural norms on dress, office hours, and language, and have as much responsible fun as possible. After the work is laid down and recognized, however, gender may enter the picture with a vengeance. The fact is, repressive societies, in their very denial of the juice that flows through all humanity, foster an unhealthy heat between bodies locked in contact all the livelong day. In an environment in which all is gray, a hint of rouge may fire an uncontrollable passion in a middle manager when a G-string and pasties in a seamy nightspot would not. A modest touch on the shoulder during a budget review may be more genuinely arousing than an authorized kiss. Where all is forbidden, everything is possible.

Very few respond to this omnipresent titillation with action. Those who do, however, experience sweet and forbidden pleasure known only to those who break all the rules while living within them. For a discussion, see **Sex**.

Good in business is not the opposite of Evil—whose existence is not officially recognized in corporate America—but simply the solid by-product of superior performance under fire. To have *done good* over the short, intermediate, or long term is the highest achievement. The attraction of the concept is its accessibility. Everyone, in his or her own way, can do good by doing well. To add to the power of the enterprise, its wealth and grandeur—that is good. And to attain personal power, wealth, and grandeur while doing so, well, that is the ultimate good, the melding of your self to the corporation, the identity of its interests with your own. Always seek to do good and you will thrive. This may be done by pleasing everyone with whom you work, from the lowest to the highest on the corporate tree. Your objective is to create a myth about yourself, an aura of excellence in its true, eternal form. Call it reputation. No man or woman can long survive without it. It is your shield against the dragon of mediocrity.

Gifts at the office should be offered only on formal occasions, accepted with aplomb and cool gratitude when appropriately offered, and, of course, given solely to those from whom you expect some benison in return. Under no circumstance should a business gift be given in friendship, for a gift is perhaps the most venal expression of servitude in business. Why else would the majority be donated to blasé executives by importunate vendors? A gift, in corporate context, is an admission of servility, or at least dependency.

The one exception to this harsh precept is the exchange of birthday keepsakes. Due to the very personal nature of such a token, it's best to keep it simple and, naturally, to pay for it yourself. The very minimalism of the gift marks it as your own—if it were more splendiferous it would be on the company tab, would it not? So a spray of flowers, or a toy gorilla, or anything that's quirky and outside the realm of the official, is an acceptable expression of natal joy in the corridors of power. Anything more will be too much, and essentially impersonal.

Gigs are all assignments that give you a chance to play some tunes and get, if not funky, at least marginally loose. It's quite useful to develop and maintain a gig mentality, viewing each task as a solid opportunity to bare your chops. Gigs have a beginning (when you arrive, set up, and get loose), a middle (when you play your heart out) and an end (when you bring the house down). Work each gig to the hilt and you'll have them standing up, hollering for more, and booking you for future dates.

Seeing your work as an assemblage of gigs is good for your soul. It beats the hell out of feeling like you're a jogging rat on a treadmill, or a tiny mote in the eye of the machine. If you've got to sweat, why not have some fun while you're at it? A hang-loose, semi-artistic, event-oriented attitude can help a lot without substantively changing your job at all. Right you are if you think you are.

Grapevine is the only place where truth forever resounds, and hence interoffice scuttlebutt is seen as the one source of unimpeachable information in the workplace. That's because speculation is always more credible, and feasible, than the current company line, which always represents the softest, most formal, least trustworthy repository of official thinking. Listen closely to the murmurs along the grapevine, since they most certainly twang with the collective wisdom of the multitudes.

H

Handshake is the initial impression you create, so make it good. There are several common misdeeds made in pressing the flesh:

• *Bone Crushing:* A leftover from the Dale Carnegie school of making friends and influencing people, which is heavily dependent on broad grins and good intentions. The pulverizing handshake usually reveals a sniveling, puling weakling overcompensating like mad, and there's no worse way to start a relationship than generating the impression that you're a dumb moose who doesn't know his own strength.

• *Wet Fish:* Amazing but true, there are still many folks who believe that grudgingly presenting you with five sodden and inert twinkies for your shaking pleasure is an adequate salutation. There is nothing more nauseating than shaking a hand that does not shake back. It makes you wonder about humanity.

• *Invasion of the Body Snatcher:* It's an equally bad idea to give the impression that you like holding hands just for fun. Remember, all good things must come to an end.

So, to avoid all the above, take the time to actually grasp the offered appendage, give a tasty squeeze, establish at least marginal eye contact, and move on. Don't pull away like you're afraid of contracting something vile. The process of disengagement should be mutual.

Finally, remember that the handshake originated in ancient days when two men wanted to show they were not armed: "Look, Ma," the greeting said, "no club." That function has not changed. The act is therefore just as necessary as an expression of good intent as it is a way to say hello. Use your handshake liberally, even with friends and good acquaintances. It gives the impression that your intentions are basically benign, even if they're not.

Headhunters are in the business of filling executive positions. Getting tapped by one is like achieving a Calvinist state of grace: either you're eligible or you're not, and no good works can get you on the A-List.

If your head is hunted, there are several proper responses, and some things to avoid. First, find out as much as possible about the firm that's hunting you before you spill your guts about your self, your hopes, and your dream position. If this means calling the firm back after an information search, so be it—better safe than sorry. More than one executive has put his name into circulation only to find his résumé on the desk of his boss. Discretion, as always, is the better part of ambition.

The key is to avoid becoming ensnared in the clutches of the middle-management meat markets, which are nothing more than glorified personnel agencies that field hundreds of applicants for thousands of mediocre jobs no more glorious than the one in which you now labor. You're looking for action from the few, high-quality firms that fill key positions you wouldn't hear of without their intervention. After you do a thorough search of the firm on your tail, you may actually be enthused about putting your head into their hat. This, however, is not the time to grovel and tell your life story. Interview the interviewer instead.

After you inquire how they got your name, try to ascertain what kind of organization they are hunting you for, the power and money of the position involved. Under no circumstances divulge, however, your exact status in return—not over the phone at least. In short, just because someone is dangling a golden carrot before your nose, don't relinquish the right to call the shots. That's not the kind of guy they're looking for.

Headquarters is the central cell of the corporate honeycomb. Those who labor there are, by definition, the heaviest hitters in the infrastructure. Not that headquarters personnel are safer, or wiser, or more individually valued. They are, however, closer to the creative core that makes the entire organism work: strategic planning and crisis management. If you work in a corporate headquarters, use your position to make life easier for the soldiers who work in the field collecting the honey. That's where the profit is made, and don't you forget it. And if you're on the outside, try to resist the impulse to see headquarters as some fusty ivory tower where gray men and women labor in pinstripe to Muzak. It's a boiler room just like yours. The mark of a good organization is a friendly working relationship between headquarters and its satellite locations. Help make that synergy happen and you'll be contributing to the well-being of the entire store. If you do that well enough, who knows? You may suddenly find yourself on your way to New York, Los Angeles, Houston, or Chicago, making a whopping urban salary that goes almost as far as your old one did, back in Pocatello, Fresno, or Des Moines.

High Profile is the ability to gain wide recognition for your activities and contributions. It's something you want to have, except when the going gets rough and it's wise to get gone. A high profile is achieved through the following means:

• *Heavy Paper:* Document your activities with enough paper (memos, letters, buckslips, etc.) to ensure that people know what you're up to. Don't try to grab all the credit, of course. Just go on record as having been integral to the birth of all projects and ideas you had a hand in.

• *You, in Their Face, Doing Something:* Keep in personal contact with all those in the organization whom you respect and need. This may mean dropping by their offices for brief chats where friendship is the only item on the agenda, lunch for no other purpose than general schmoozing, or, sometimes, active solicitation of projects. Whatever it takes, don't let them forget you're alive. That's one short step from not being alive.

• *We Deliver:* That should be the message you send to

anyone who utilizes your services or that of your department. Send no one away unsatisfied.

Of course, when trouble flares, your high profile can make you the first one called to extinguish the blaze. And a bad scene may rebound to your discredit simply because you're a large target. This is the price you pay for maintaining a respectable niche.

Hiring is a pleasant task—just make sure you do it right. You can raise your odds of selecting the right person by working hard to draft a truthful job description beforehand, then being totally honest with every applicant about the nature of the post in question, its limitations, challenges, and potential for growth. Don't believe you can mold a lump of meat into an ice sculpture, either. What you see at the interview is often more than what you're going to get. And when an important job is on the line, interview the final suitors more than once, maybe more than twice. You're going to have to live with the new person—wrongful firing rules being what they are—for a good long time. And remember, their performance is a comment on your good judgment, or lack thereof.

Hitman is an extraordinarily heavy weapon the corporation points at excess head count, an individual dedicated to nothing but the eradication of those who are so firmly entrenched in the works—by seniority, numbers, or both—that only Herculean measures will blast them loose. In short, he fires people. The hitman is invariably new to the organization and has no loyalties to mire his feet in sentiment. He is given the charter to "restructure" the company, or to "realize operating efficiencies," or, perhaps, "simply to look us over from top to bottom and suggest some changes that will ensure our continued profitable growth." Whatever. He's there to execute enough people to justify his worth.

Endangered species under his scrutiny (which means everyone but the guy who hired him) can take comfort in the fact that, like every executioner, he will be gone when his job is done. Until then, treat him with respectful reserve, and stay out of his way as much as possible. Neither his enmity nor his friendship will do you any good. The first will mean your extinction when he gets an inspiration on how to further streamline things; the second will mean your doom as the hitman is expelled from the healthy corporate body when his work is done. When the big bad wolf is dead, everyone takes justifiable pleasure in kicking his former friends and associates down the stairs. So keep clear of the carnage. Sometimes it's nice to be Switzerland.

Hobbies are often the sole link between a workaholic and his humanity. They are also a terrific door opener when you're looking for conversation with a guy whose idea of chat is idle comment on projected cash-flow differentials. The more elevated the executive, the more entranced he usually is with his antique guns, boats in bottles, boats out of bottles, toy banks, prune farming, you name it: every driven manager has a secret and well-financed passion that makes life bearable when he is forced to be away from the office for brief periods of time. Get him to talk about it, and you'll have found the key to his private little heart.

Hotels can be places in which to get a good night's sleep, or dens of iniquity in which to misbehave. You're far from home, living like a king off plastic, and totally incognito. Don't let it go to your head, especially if there are colleagues around. Getting a name as a wild and crazy guy is marginally acceptable, especially in entrepreneurial organizations. Earning a reputation as a drunk and a "sex maniac" is never acceptable for a guy in charge of a seven-figure budget line. So be good. And if you can't, be careful.

Humor can be the greatest asset you bring to any interface. Fortunately, you don't have to be Woody Allen to kill a corporate audience. Just the mere intimation of wit often sends a room of hitherto gloomy executives into paroxysms of laughter. Punch lines like, "It certainly is," or "No kidding, Jack," can wrest a torrent of hilarity from a somber room, causing senior management to remove hankies and wipe their eyes from the surfeit of sheer amusement.

The sorry fact is that business is a deeply serious occupation, and the issues under discussion often range from the grave to the merely bleak, so the simple intention of cracking a joke is generally appreciated, even marveled at. If you've got the gift to amuse, use it, if only to cast a lighter perspective on the proceedings. It will be one more reason for key management to invite you to crucial gatherings, and a good way to make yourself not only welcome, but an invaluable addition to the chemistry of the event.

I

Image is what you appear to be. It is one level more superficial than that jewel, reputation, and it's the easiest thing in the world to achieve if you don't try too hard. Dress sharp—not like a fop, of course, but to generate the impression that you wear the uniform with pride and creativity. Smile whenever you can, and, above all else, look each man and woman in the eye when you talk to them. It doesn't hurt to seal every key exchange with a gesture of friendship—a touch on the shoulder on the way out the door, an impulsively extended hand that cannot be denied, even a moderately serious salute to a fellow officer—anything to warm the air with a vague aura of conviviality and mutual regard. It is also a good idea to project a sense that you have too much to do because you are so essential to so many revenue streams. This is smoothly done, too, if you limit bullshitting with your friends and associates to small, intense bursts, rather than long, foot-on-the-credenza gabfests.

Finally, be sure that your image is flavored with just a little bit of your real personality, i.e., your faults. It's hard to trust a man who shows none, and you'll flake out in no time if you don't evince a bit of gristle to the public eye. So retain your right to be grumpy under pressure, taciturn when tired, or garrulous when slightly in your cups. Don't, of course, flaunt traits and opinions that would be totally unacceptable to your corporation, like, say, uncontrolled drug addiction, pederasty on company time, or belief in trade unionism. An image is a terrible thing to waste.

Imagination begins with the ability to ask questions, simple ones like "What if?" and "Why not?" The rational mind plays its part, sure, as critic, evaluator, censor, and eventually salesman. But the nonrational mind has to kick in, too, or no idea comes, since they are the ultimate by-product of an active imagination. Ideas are not all you need—it helps to have guts, grit, and guile to back them up—but they're mighty useful.

Contrary to popular belief, there is no such thing as an "imaginative type" as opposed to an "analytical type," so don't let yourself be pigeonholed. Everyone has imagination, and all talented people know how to use theirs. In order to gain access to your imagination, however, you're going to have to arrange thinking time for yourself. Good ideas occasionally come while you're trotting down the hall to that seventh meeting of the day, but the vast majority materialize out of the ether when you're bowling, or munching something tasty, or staring at the ceiling without a thought in your head. Make time for some of that. It's just as sure an investment in your future as attending that industry hobnob next month.

In-Box is the repository of all you're supposed to have a handle on. Unfortunately, an in-box is often a horizontal garbage can, a bottomless pit from which no paper ever emerges. This simply won't do. If you have a stack in your in-box the size of the Yellow Pages, get vicious with yourself and ream it out. In the process, you're sure to find a plethora of once-critical situations you comfortably ignored, then repressed altogether. So what? If they haven't already snuck up and bitten you in the rear, they probably were fictitious anyway. Toss that paper. The stuff you have to keep for future reference, file. The invariably slim sheaf of material that represents the detritus of actual work-in-progress may now comfortably rest in your now pristine in-box for immediate action and ultimate removal to— where else?—your out-box.

Insincerity is a nasty way of putting it. Some people just call it being polite, and count it a virtue. The fact is, the ability to feel one thing and say another is the cornerstone of civilization. Be prepared to share your true thoughts with anyone who sincerely asks, naturally, but a deep commitment to telling people exactly where you're at, at all times, went out with the 1970s, except in California. So be glib when you have to, and some of the time when you don't, and save your sincerity for when it counts, in the clinches. People will appreciate the effort you're making to keep things friendly and not too personal. Don't, of course, go around bent over double, gibbering greasy flatteries and jocularities. Good manners are invisible.

Intercom is the communications system within a department, the means of keeping in touch without having to bump into your peers every ten minutes. Classically, it's a button on your phone that lights up and buzzes when, say, you've got a joker on the line your secretary wants you to know about. It is therefore an important aid in ducking unwanted calls, which is essential for efficient work. In other cases, use your intercom for communications of ten words or less, such as, "The Kramer papers stink. See me," or "Sorry to hear you're going to jail." Intercoms are not tools for extended negotiation or heavy interpersonal relating. If you use them to excess, your mates will think you fear or loathe to meet them face-to-face. Which, even if true, is an unfortunate, not to say unpopular, thing to convey.

Interfacing is a terrific word that has come down to us from Computerland. It means what it looks like—two faces coming together, or, conversely, someone in your face. The word should always be used with a sense of humor, since only nerds use computer lingo in human conversation without smirking. But Corporate English is rich. Those who use it with flair have one more tool in the fight for successful interfacing.

International Relations demand extensive research
and preparation. It will be necessary for you to learn the mores,
quirks, and cultural demands of your host country if you expect to do any successful business there. Speaking to people in
their language, eating their food without gagging, and accepting
with grace their potentially odd notions of hospitality is an
acquired skill. So if you're assigned a gig overseas, debrief an
expert—preferably someone who has been there recently—on
the appropriate protocol. That way you won't blow a deal in
Tokyo because you refused to eat a live lobster as it waved at
you with all sixteen feelers, or irrevocably alienate a Berber by
showing him the bottom of your shoes, or enrage an Inuit by
refusing to dance closely with his wife. Sure, the things you
may have to do to convince an international businessman of
your good intentions may be alien to your nature, but the
potential benefits justify the effort. It may be comforting to
contemplate the fact that this assimilation of strange customs,
traditions, and values is, in essence, no different from the
process of dealing successfully with IBM or General Electric,
whose cultures are probably just as foreign to most civiliza-
tions as we know them. So buckle down and learn the rules you
need to win.

Intrapreneur is a buzzword coined to describe all those
inside a corporate hierarchy who behave with the same gutsy
personal resolve evinced by dynamic, creative empire builders.
Why it has suddenly become necessary to distinguish "intras"
from "entres" is anyone's guess. The new word, however, man-
dates the creation of another. Since intrapreneurs are, in effect,
inner entrepreneurs, their opposites, clearly, must be those
who function in classic fashion outside the corporate structure,
i.e., "extra" preneurially. Thus we have three nouns—entre-,
intra-, and extrapreneurs—where before just one sufficed.
That's 300 percent growth, a handsome success rate in any
business, even language.
    It's important not to get seduced by the baroque use of
verbiage prevalent in business culture. New words are constantly created to describe the same simple things. This, in

turn, generates a comforting sensation of forward momentum, development, and growth. Keep your eye on the reality underneath the designer terms. The guy who builds a hundred-million-dollar project out of nothing, whether he is inside, outside, under, or around the organization, is an entrepreneur, with the guts and scars to show for it. If that's you, congratulations. If it's not, get in line behind him, or get out of his way. He's going places.

Investment is money spent with the expectation of a return. The money you get back is referred to as the *return on investment,* or *ROI*. Properties that do not contribute a good ROI within the projected time frame suffer divestiture. And that's the bottom line.

Japanese Management is a fictional conceit that means a lot more to the American consumer of business journalism than to the average Japanese, who does not read *Business Week*. The essence of true Japanese management is the nullity of the individual, the dedication to zero defects from top to bottom of the organization, the total unity of each worker with the aims of the whole, and the absence of thoroughly Occidental ambition in any participating units within the infrastructure except for senior management. Absolutely essential to this utopia is the unquestioned superiority of Management Über Alles. Japanese workers are reportedly pleased to labor without promotion for decades. Now that's dedication.

Once such patriotic acquiescence is established, it becomes very easy to ask whether individual workers prefer white toilet paper to mauve in the regional rest rooms, or whether a zorn flange would be a better ion medium than zircon alloy in nipple conductors nationwide. This is what they call participatory management, and it's the puff pastry around the autocratic Japanese model that has caught the fancy of the business media that American management reads. Don't be conned if a deep thinker in business planning begins touting the Nipponese model. American workers are not of the inscrutable East, and selflessness is not considered an unequivocal virtue in these

United States. Those who advocate it should be viewed with suspicion, if not alarm. Big Brother may not be watching yet, but he's darned interested.

Jargon refers to words people use instead of saying what they mean, perhaps because they in fact mean nothing. Like any enjoyable bad habit, it must be mastered and controlled, lest it turn you into a jerk on wheels. Current examples of pure jargon include "impact" as a verb, as in, "That alternative will impact me negatively in a number of key areas." Evident here, aside from the flatulent tone, is the classic superfluity of good jargon. The previous remark could, of course, be rendered in traditional English as, "No thanks." The jargon is used to masquerade the transparent banality of the thought, to dress it up and give it the patina of rational discourse. Derivations include "impacted" (in a postdental sense), and the amazing "impactful," as in, "Your work has been impactful here, Jack. Congratulations."

Other trendy examples abound, gleaning terminology from virtually all disciplines. To get someone's opinion these days, you've got to have him "focus" (optics) on whether you're properly "positioned" (marketing) to "win" (sports). Make sure to thank him afterward for his "feedback" (Jimi Hendrix). Perhaps most omnipresent these days is the pernicious, computer-based "interface," as in "I love interfacing with you, Mort, you're a real team player." The word immediately places human relations squarely into the realm where people trade data and nobody feels any pain.

In addition to simple dumb lingo, mandatory jargon also includes your Big Concepts, terms that attain popularity, only to disappear into obsolescence like verbal hula hoops. Jargon of this order fuels the business publishing industry, which has feasted on words like productivity, commitment, and excellence since Dale Carnegie taught Walter Mitty how to make friends and influence people.

To get by with jargoneers, you will also need those special words native to your particular industry, its technology, and its coded messages. These are the aforementioned buzzwords, and they, too, are evanescent as mayflies and twice as fecund.

Overuse of jargon is a sure indication of a tiny mind at work. A little recreational indulgence, however, generally elicits an appreciative snort and chuckle. It works best for those who serve it up lean, with a sprig of irony. And under no circumstances should it be employed outside your office, where its terrifying vacuity is on display for all to hear.

Job is the phalanx of tasks that luck, fate, and your manager decree your hours are meant for. It is a lot more than a collection of assignments. It's the sum total of what you contribute to your corporate culture. So never cut an "is not my yob" posture unless you're prepared to cede that authority, the attendant headaches, and potential glory, to someone else. If you abdicate too often, the general population will come to regard you as a functionary with a highly circumscribed role. Better to be known as a slightly exploited Jack-of-all-gigs, prepared to take on whatever assignments the wind and other people's wisdom, laziness, or ineptitude blow your way. As your superb capabilities become known, you'll be building an ongoing case for your indispensability, perhaps the most important fiction in your arsenal. For the skill that makes every job a potential stepping-stone, see **Prioritizing.**

Job Description is the internal document that outlines your formal responsibilities; it exists somewhere in the depths of your personal file. Get a gander at it about three months before your next performance review and note any errors— either of omission or commission—between the neat description of your duties and the dirty job you are actually doing. This disparity is your guarantee of promotability.

For instance, if your job description says you "assist the president in the preparation of the annual report," and you, in fact, wrote, edited, designed, oversaw the $275,000 production job and supervised distribution, you've got an excellent case for an increase in salary and title. An inaccurate job description shows how far you've come since it was written and, maybe, what you're worth.

Job Interview is a direct-sales task, pure and simple, so don't be squeamish about pushing the product. In this case, the customer is in the market for a human being. Happily, that's exactly what you're selling. Hard or soft, each good salesperson has a relentless, indomitable sense of personal style, so go with the pace and energy level that make you comfortable. That's probably what you do best, anyway.

The primary goal of any job interview is to show yourself, which, naturally, is what makes the experience so tough. Face it, it's quite possible they won't like you, maybe even probable. You've certainly got your quirks. Nevertheless, there is no percentage in concealing your basic identity. There are few things more likely to produce transcendental desperation than a bad job, one in which the best part of your self goes to sleep eight hours a day, or forever. So be just the way you are. Who knows, the guy might surprise you and accept you on your own terms, just as if you were a real adult.

Remember, too, that, while you don't have to slam backs like a borscht-belt schmoozer, your approach should be crafted to the guy interviewing you. Does he need to be jogged from a coma? Soothed out of paranoid jitters? Entertained? People who are good at selling themselves (or selling shaving cream, for that matter) are those who can forge at least a temporary illusion of fellowship and the need, in the customer, to validate that relationship with a purchase. Creating such intimacy means, in part, listening, so don't be afraid to keep the interviewer gabbing. Talking is half the fun of interviewing, and while he's holding forth, he just might give you a real peek at the organization you seek to serve.

If you want the job, though, don't be too cool and professional to make a blatant pitch for yourself. Tell your life story, and try to make it interesting, if not exciting. Express passion about your prior career, your hobbies, your kids. And somewhere in the waning minutes of the meet, transmit the clear impression that you're interested in the job and think you could do very well at it—if you are and if you could. Confidence and ambition are never out of place; in fact, they're what the interviewer wants to hear. Keep in mind that he's as desperate as you are to see that slot filled by someone with manifest talent and drive. He simply has to find out that person is you.

One last thing: when it's over, briefly consider how things could have gone better, and worse, and then forget about it. You've done what you could to get the job. The rest is up to them. If they have perspicacity, courage, and wit, they will select you. If they do not, you'll continue interviewing firms until you find one who does.

Jokes are generally as Not Funny in business as they are everywhere else, with the possible exception of the Catskills. You still, of course, have to know how to make them. With some execs, especially beancounters, numbers and jokes may be the only words you can share. So practice a few funny darts for delivery. You won't need more than four per quarter, unless you're a compulsive yukster. Before you tell a joke, consider:

• *Selection:* Keep a keen eye out for business humor that you think would tickle the general fancy. Since many big cheeses read nothing but correspondence and Tom Peters megatomes, citations from virtually all media may be safely quoted without fear of seeming stale. Cartoons and quips from *The New Yorker,* for instance, are an invaluable source of yuks for corporate officers. Farther from cosmopolitan headquarters, *Reader's Digest* excels as a rich source of amusing anecdote. Best of all, however, are jokes that have nothing to do with anything. Verbatim quotes from Jay Leno, stolen from last night's "Tonight Show," are absolutely devastating before a corporate audience. Don't be too nice about revealing your sources, either. Theft of quality material is a show-business tradition.

Unless you travel with a stupid bunch of yahoos, never tell a slurpy racist, ethnic, or sexist joke, unless the joke is on your race, ethnicity, or sex. If you should venture into the "how many Polacks, Jews, and elderly Negro gentlemen does it take to change a light bulb" genre, make sure you're hanging around with your kind of people. And although a certain amount of profanity is not only permissible but advisable, never deliver a grossly obscene joke except in the company of men who share your level of maturity. Keep in mind that few dirty jokes are funny in the light of day. And that guys who tell a lot of them generally have trouble getting laid.

• *Placement:* There is most certainly a wrong time for jokes—like in the middle of a budget review in which you're being instructed to cut your department by 40 percent. The more formalized the situation, in fact, the less likely an unwritten joke will be appropriate. The punishment for bad placement is immediate and devastating—public bombing. Choose to launch your joke when it can be slipped into the prevailing jocularity like a banana peel under the collective foot. If you have to ask yourself whether it's the right moment to tell one, it probably isn't.

• *Delivery:* Books have been written on this subject, and not one of them has been useful to guys who have no talent to amuse. A joke should be embarked on with good energy, told with dispatch, and closed with a flourish. It's not called a punch line for nothing, so hit it like you expect at least polite laughter. There's nothing more devastating than postjoke silence, except, perhaps, the solitary voice raised in the query, "You mean that's it?"

If you aren't any good, step aside and let the more practiced and compulsive among you do the telling. It's no shame to be unable to wreak a laugh from what is, essentially, the most rudimentary form of humor beyond the whoopie cushion. You may be one of those who can only field a wry riposte, or a canny barb. Know the form of humor that works best for you and run with it. Your friends will thank you.

Finally, never fail to distinguish mere jokery from its deep, mysterious, far more interesting mother, wit.

Jumping Ship is what everyone does when they have the chance, but that doesn't mean it's a pretty thing to watch. It's only natural for those who used to lunch you and punch you to avert their eyes when word gets out you were snatched up for obscene bucks by a firm they hate. Jumping ship isn't simply polite departure from an old friend, it's a sad act laden with promises tossed aside, and yes, it feels a little bit like treason.

But it's not, not really. It's just a display of rank self-interest. That's behavior no corporation is entitled to criticize, and anyone who claims otherwise is a little cracked.

The term itself is seldom used by a happy company, whose success is usually so institutionalized that every man is replaceable by an approximation of himself. In entrepreneurial or wobbly management organizations, though, an individual can still make a big difference, and abandonment of his appointed role, especially for lucre, strikes at the very deepest and most heartfelt illusion of a corporation, i.e., that it's a family. No matter how hard it tries to be one, however, it isn't, and you need not die in its arms. No family pays you money to see you eight or twelve hours a day, and your mother cannot fire you for being obnoxious. Companies give you money in exchange for your most precious commodity, the one that can never be replenished: time. And if you're not moving to achieve your absolute limit in this particular life span, you're wasting it.

Central to a truly ambitious and successful career is the maintenance of the delusion that one's life is a magnificent journey without historic precedent, a saga whose future lies somewhere in the mists that cling to the snowcapped heights. Acceptance of the opposite—that you are exactly where God intended you to be and are, in fact, somewhat satisfied—is the clarion of early middle age.

Your real friends and family will make the plunge with you. The rest will be left behind. If that prospect seems unspeakable, maybe it's time to think about sticking around. Maybe money is not that important to you, or power. Maybe all you need is love.

K

Kicked Upstairs is the fate of those who achieve great size in both success and years of service, who are, in some crucial way, still an integral part of the organization that desperately seeks to run without them. These are usually once-potent forces who—due to stubborn personal style, advanced age, bad politics, or simply the need to make room for the next generation of managers—must be deprived of the pleasures and pressures of daily office through upward, not downward, expulsion. It might simply be his resonant, parental presence, either benign or terrifying, that lends the company its depth, history, and sense of mission, and also slows it down. He may enjoy an elderly power base that cannot be dispensed with except by attrition, or death, whichever comes first. To ease the beloved dinosaur into the tar pit, management must afford him a plump post with no authority.

Thus we see a bustling president puffed into an impotent chairman with a staff of two; a chairman hoisted into a lonely chief executive's chair from which he is free to take an infinite lunch and to play with his paper clips; the staunch CEO promoted to the arcane new position of executive chairman of a board, which, unfortunately for him, meets but once a year in an advisory role. Whatever the terminology, the effect is clear to all: the guy has died and gone to management heaven, from whence he can see all and affect nothing.

In rare cases, a viable middle manager will find himself offered a juicy false promotion. This must be tossed back like a working grenade—with solid, cool, and deliberate aim. The guy offering you that executive vice-presidency with indeterminate duties is not a friend, even when he speaks of the "magnificent challenge" the position offers, or how you can "write your own ticket as far as where you want to take it." Keep your current, explicit duties and muster those around you who value your performance. You're going to need them. Getting kicked upstairs means you're in the way of someone with a Big Agenda, one who would rather buy you than fight you. When he finds you're not for sale, watch out.

Naturally, if all things go against you, and you're staring at the possibility of actually writing that novel in the bountiful spare time that comes with unemployment, you may want to accept the kick upstairs and wait for your moment. Who knows, the power structure that unseated you may falter. Vacuums may open through which you could reenter in triumph, like Napoleon or something. Or, if push comes to shove, you might be able to make yourself such a pain in the keester you're suddenly eligible for your ticket to perpetual ease. For a discussion, see **Parachute.**

Kicking Ass is good exercise, but those who abuse the privilege may find their own in the broaster. For, while most of us need swift contact now and then, and recognize its justice when righteously administered, we want to be able to resume our duties with dignity intact. Guys who boot you down the block and enjoy it are dead meat in your book from that time forth, period. Remember that fact when you're teeing up, and go for the onside kick, not the punt.

When yours is the target, take a long moment to evaluate whether you've earned this thumping. If you forgot the quarterly confab with security analysts and the chairman entered without the results of the fall-quarter audit, and was humiliated, don't expect to sit down without a pillow for a couple of weeks, if you're lucky. In fact, a thorough ass-kicking can be a good sign you're really not out of favor. You always hurt the one you love, especially when he spits up on your shoes.

If, on the other hand, you gave the chairman's aide the aforementioned report and his dog ate them, block that kick with a little calm information. Why be a glutton for punishment?

Kudos are official plaudits, and they do come, occasionally. Don't minimize their import, and never fail to say thank you to the guy who has gone on the record to say you're great. When the vice-president of finance sends you a thank-you note for your "banzaii" help on the twelve-year strategic plan, and sends copies to most of the civilized world, call him up and tell him he's a class act, because he is. When the CEO in Toledo makes a thirty-second dive bomb into your speakerphone to congratulate you for a big deal, match his admiration with your own—of him, and his generosity. The corporate world is full of people hoarding praise unto themselves like starving men secreting stale crusts of bread in their bedclothes. Guys who like you a lot and are prepared to show it are what makes this country great. Water them, and they will grow.

And by the way, save those gold stars in a little file marked "Kudos." They can make for toasty reading later on, in good times and bad.

Laughter is a gift that should be dispensed with full generosity of spirit. This is because it's rarely earned. When a gag, quip, or riposte doesn't work, and your face is about to fail to laugh, it may be necessary to perform an act just as skillful as the guy who laid the egg on you. There are three acceptable responses that will get you out of this spot without excessive dishonesty or, worse, rudeness:

• *Har-har-har:* The oldest business tool is still one of the best. Corporate laughter, like laughter in a bad production of *Love's Labors Lost,* is a little too lusty, and can be easily replicated by those who feel nothing, but wish to seem jocular. If you can indicate a level of mirth sufficient to bend you double and postpone sentient speech for a few moments, so much the better. The attempt to feign a positive response will be appreciated, even if it is not totally successful. And, if the joke was a real stinker, feel free to exclaim, "Bad joke, Jack! Congratulations!" A truly terrible joke is often a great one in disguise.

• *Heh-heh-heh:* The polite chuckle is a dignified standby, too, and should be employed if a larger response would seem overly insincere, especially in a group. It is very helpful, if you're able, to convey the distinct impression that the joke was far too *true* to be laughed at with disrespectful verve.

• *Hmm . . . :* Sometimes a joke is so vague, or so ineptly presented, that the punch line sneaks up and knocks you dazed before you have a chance to forge a simulated laugh. In such cases, summon up a facial expression of wondrous admiration, place a soft hand on the offending shoulder, and offer something kind and clinical like, "Good joke, Henry, outstanding joke. Wherever did you pick it up?" You may actually want to take the time to learn it. Sure, it's a clunker, but you'll make the guy feel better, and who knows—the joke just might come in handy at the next sitdown of the marketing squad.

Ultimately, though, no technique will help you loosen your guts and let it rip. The attempt to make a laugh is one of the sole humanizing elements of business life. It should be a source of joy, not shame. So don't be a tough house—laugh!

Laziness is the reward for a desk well cleared. Treasure the days when your phone lies dormant and the interoffice mail is light, and use them to unwind in luxuriant laziness without remorse. A day or two exploring used-book shops, reading the business press, and catching up on your long-term telephone relationships is time well spent. You'll use those recharged batteries plenty when things are bonkers again.

Institutionalized laziness, on the other hand, when pursued as an ongoing policy by a seasoned practitioner, is the scourge of all busy organizations. A lazy person inflicts atrophy by chilling action on live projects until they freeze over. The good news is that sooner or later, they are *gone,* simply because one too many projects lies stillborn in their arms. Pick and choose the times you want to goof off, and make sure there's nothing pending that might make your private vacation a public scandal.

If you find yourself forced to squeeze work out of a lazy peer, subordinate, or superior, remember that the ability to nap while those around you are sweating blood is seldom considered a virtue by those who run the show. This is a fact known to even the most lethargic. Few execs will respond to a direct call to action with a yawn and a remark like, "Gosh, Ted, I really wanted to be lazy this week. Can you call me next Friday?" Set harsh deadlines with the sloth and keep up an oppressive level of pressure. He'll be only too happy to initiate a flurry of activity just to get you off his case. Don't, of course, expect top-drawer stuff. You can't get blood from a drone.

Letterhead is stationery with your name and title on it. The sense of job security and solidity it provides may be largely illusory (throwing away others' dead paper is a deeply revered aspect of corporate life), but formal letterhead is an expected part of the trappings of office. So keep it current as your title improves, and use it in good health for all communications with anyone outside your walls. As people with letterhead of their own, they might not take you 100 percent seriously on anonymous lightweight bond. Never use it for internal correspondence, of course. That's why God invented buckslips.

Leverage is a very complicated concept, but it's one of those words that make you sound savvy, so work it a bit when you're partying with nonfinancial types. Most won't even ask you what you mean when you say, "I hear Savoyard is engineering a leveraged buyout of Oxymoron," since they expect quite rightly that enduring the explanation is a far worse fate than continued ignorance. When pressed, however, you may say that leverage is the process of buying things with debt, not money. Only the very rich can try it, capable, as they are, of managing great accumulations of both.

If you're a T. Booner, leverage may mean obtaining a massive loan to gobble up a vulnerable company, offering no cash down and no collateral but your pretty face and *the assets of the acquired company*. The monthly payments to your jolly banker are met—you guessed it—with the new company's cash flow. Notice that none of *your* money has been sullied. This ability to buy strictly on the strength of the proposed management's credibility also enables an *existing* regime to sculpt plans by which they can stave off unfriendly mergers by buying their own firm. Either way, you're playing with funny money, with the creative banker at the fulcrum.

Firms are also said to be "highly leveraged" if they can build revenue without incurring additional costs. In the operation of a utility, for instance, major investment has already been made—in pipeline, telephone pole, whatever—and each new customer's monthly check goes almost entirely to the bottom line. If you run a butcher shop, however, each rib roast that leaves your store must be replaced at substantial cost to you, not to mention the cow. This cuts down on the ratio between expenses and revenues. For a discussion of this concept, see **Margin.**

Logo is the little symbol that represents your company. Every firm that advertises, even in the most cursory way, has one. For some, it's just the name emblazoned in all its formality and majesty. Others elicit associations more lush and evocative: screaming eagles, strutting roosters, big, bold initials floating within glowing mandalas, horned gods encircled by stars. A good logo is as permanent as the institution it stands for, and a firm toys with it at its peril. Your logo is you, and those who criticize it are basically telling you that they don't like your face.

If, however, your enterprise is undergoing much-needed revitalization, or has recently been acquired by a wise and benevolent parent, a new logo can be just the thing to cement your refurbished image and operating mentality both inside and outside the organization. Don't try to dream it up yourself. Expect to pay top dollar for the talents of a visionary able to symbolize your gestalt with insight born of distance. Your mysterious and beautiful corporate culture demands no less.

Long-term Project is a specific management challenge. A task whose due date stretches off into the next quarter can seem very far away until suddenly you need to deliver the goods posthaste and all you've got are babbled excuses about sluggish vendors. Such a failure will immediately target you as one who is incapable of senior status, since people at the highest levels deal almost exclusively with projects of elephantine weight and duration.

Your first step, as with any assignment, is to receive a specific due date. "Sometime next summer" may serve well as the title for a teen movie, but it doesn't do much for your strategic planning. When you've made them nail it down, plan your various duties and their target dates carefully, with profound reverence for Murphy's invariable law. Let your surprises come when things go right, not like they usually do.

Your planning done, relax and start at the beginning. Work the project in intense installments, but don't let it take over until the very end. In fact, there's little reason to get all hot and sticky about any phase of a long-term project, since, if you've got it by the throat, each of its parts is manageable, even fun. While it comes together, you may even put it on a back burner, keeping a keen eye on whether it's cooking nicely, burning, or boiling over. Serve it up when it's congealed, and voilà.

There is one personal vice that can single-handedly spoil the entire process—the working man's old friend, procrastination.

Love at the office is a wonderful, if transient thing, and don't let party poopers tell you differently. The saucy tang of naughty indiscretion adds bite to the affair, and the ferocity of unchained emotion is thrown into high relief by the drab environment in which it has exploded. Like all romances that take root in a highly specialized world, however, your office love may not survive transplantation into the real world of other social milieux, other cities, other jobs. So enjoy it while it lasts, and if it lasts forever, bravo. And don't mind the giggles and glee of your peers as the reality of the situation begins to dawn on them. Though they dress like undertakers, people in business are no more mature than anyone else about matters of the major organs. Repress the urge, naturally, to rub their noses in your happiness.

And keep in mind that your most public love affair, if you wish to maintain your reputation as a key player and not some love-struck chump, must be with your work. No other love—for sweetheart, spouse, friend, or child—must be allowed to diminish the public passion you evince for your job. That's the only affair the corporation really cares to know about. The rest, as far as it's concerned, is gossip.

Loyalty is a terrific personal attribute, highly regarded in all cultures, for where loyalty does not exist, the naked face of business is revealed in all its stark, self-absorbed brutality. Beneath the veneer of warmth and jolly cheer, a corporation is organized to do certain things if it does no other: to make money, to perpetuate itself unto a thousand generations, and to grow like a weed. To do this efficiently over more than one lifetime, it must transcend the concerns of the impermanent mortals who, for now, operate it. Its ultimate loyalty has been and always must be to itself.

This rampaging sense of organizational egotism naturally radiates from the center of the corporation into the soul of every person, no matter how benign or altruistic you may want to be. To the extent your interests are one with those of your co-workers and your company, you, they, and it may be blithely loyal to each other. It certainly does make life easier to believe that you and your cohorts are All In This Thing Together. And most of the time, you will be.

Your first and most pressing loyalty is to the people you labor side by side with every day: your peers, clients, and allies. Your loyalty to them need only be made up of the simplest, most durable stuff: honest hard work and good information. Deliver on time and under budget and you'll be loyal in the very deepest sense—by helping them do their jobs better.

Your loyalty to your boss is a much more complicated beast. Recognize that your two fortunes are, for better or worse, intertwined. More than one perfectly viable colonel has eaten dirt when his general was cashiered. You've got to be a second set of senses for your boss and view his interests as your own. Listen at meetings for folks who are preparing to kneecap him, or to skirt his influence. Defend his programs, his record, and even his honor, if necessary. In short, run interference. People will think well of you, don't worry, even if they hate his guts. Professional allegiance looks good on just about everybody.

If, however, you see his ship of office foundering (and you, not he, may be first to hear the confirmation), don't carry loyalty to the point of stupidity. No one expects you to descend into the maelstrom willingly, not even your boss, if he still has his wits about him. Self-preservation is the ultimate, most comprehensible motivation of every business organism, including you. Those who hang in there against all expectations are afforded the greatest regard in the gray halls. They're called survivors.

This doesn't mean you have to help the prevailing winds blow your boss away. In these dark days, your loyalty can be best expressed by continued good work in his behalf and, as the storm gathers force, simple friendship. At the same time, begin spreading the understanding in the larger community that you are your own person, with a future not necessarily linked to the drowning manager whose failures have suddenly made you an endangered species.

In so doing, you will be expressing fealty to the largest master of them all: the vast, impersonal machine that exploits your talents and pays your rent.

Lunch is a perfectly serviceable business institution that has been allowed to bloat into a behemoth of unmanageable size, frequency, and duration by professional hedonists who have elevated its marginal status to Olympian proportions. When all is said and done, lunch is often more useful for networking and chat than it is for actual labor. These things have their place, but they sure shouldn't take a third of the working day, or make you fat unless you want to be. For further discussion, see **Eating.**

M

Mail Room is the digestive system of the company—taking in information, processing it, and spitting it out again—and when it clogs, the organization, for all its brains, heart, and many-fisted work force, grinds to a screeching halt. Memos with precious clearance disappear into unseen hoppers, never to emerge; reports demanded by field locations are sent flying to erroneous postal zones; requests for action languish in limbo. In short, the vitality of the corporation, which lies, most of all, in good communication with itself, founders.

Fortunately, few mail rooms are totally fouled up, although most perpetually perch on the brink of meltdown, staffed, as they are, by guys who sincerely couldn't care less about the day-to-day priorities that swirl around them. These are the groundlings, and few, except at the William Morris Agency, have any chance to reach mainstream white-collar affluence and self-satisfaction. This gives them a dangerous sense of proportion about the demands of scurrying, get-ahead types that are constantly barking up their tree.

To get the most out of your mail room, begin by cultivating a friendly relationship with the senior manager. Take the time to shoot the breeze with the guy and let him know that you think his job is important, and difficult. When you have a particularly hairy communication going out or coming in, ask him to handle it personally. He'll appreciate the trust. Most people think he has the IQ of a houseplant and treat him just that way. And don't forget him when you're compiling your booze list at holiday time. You just might be the only guy who remembers.

Make an effort, too, to get to know his team on a first-name basis, and to treat them not as mindless androids, but as regular joes with a grody job to do—just like you.

Major Fuck-Up is the monster that lurks on the dark side of your dreams. It is a breakdown of prodigious magnitude in which your personal malfeasance, laziness, or stupidity—or those of a person or persons under your aegis—creates a problem that may hurt the entire company. They are endured, eventually, by almost everyone. Some of us even survive them.

The key lies in differentiating the major from the everyday. When the scratch sheets from your annual budget review are understandably mistaken for garbage by the office cleaning service, leaving you without the mandatory notation to back up your argument, that is not a fuck-up, major or minor. That's just a common snafu, which usually can be righted with a whimsical explanation and polite apology. Not so when the budget itself, along with your department's financial records for the past decade, fall overboard on the ferry to Martha's Vineyard because you chose to review them during a long weekend at the beach. In such an awesome eventuality, the active principle is that *you are guilty,* and that no excuse or apology will repair the damage.

So don't offer any. To babble when your actions, or those of your staff, have been beyond defense, is to beg for retribution. Better to gather your dignity about you, throw yourself on the mercy of those who hold your fate in their angry little hands, and hope your prior record will speak loudly for itself. It will be harder for your tormentor to punish you as roundly as he'd anticipated if you're in the process of flaying yourself with superior gusto. You may even go so far as to offer your resignation, if you're sure it won't be accepted.

If it's one of your underlings who dropped the blimp, resist the urge to make that your public excuse. There are few things more contemptible to decent folk than a guy who shoots his subordinates when things go sour. You are, after all, as responsible for your staff as you are for yourself; even more so, since failure of your people is a comment not only on your performance, but on your management skills. Whipping your troops will simply make you look like a worm as well as a fuck-up.

This is not to say, however, that your guilty parties—if they exist—should escape inviolate while you are being torched. After you take your lumps, descend on the miscreant in the comfort and privacy of your office or, if his sin is great, in an open meeting. If he grovels the way you did, forgive him in the same spirit that recently spared your life. If he enjoys absolutely no insight into the dimensions of his crime and peppers you with a rain of lame rationalizations, this is proof that the offender may be a recidivist. With staff like that, you don't need enemies.

Managing is a simple but rigorous craft, like wheelwrighting. If you follow certain clear-cut steps, you have managed. This is a good thing. The opposite of managing is reacting. Reacting is neither a fruitful way of approaching a given project, nor your job on the whole. When you manage, you take control of the welter of long-term assignments, crises, opportunities, power plays, and pitfalls that confront you every day. When you do not manage but merely react, you may succeed on sheer moxie and smarts for a long, long time. But eventually, the lack of operational structure in your work will wash over you like a flood, and you will drown.

Project management may be broken down into five steps:

• *Mission Control:* To focus your work, you need an Objective. It may be something concrete like, "Prepare a list of the company's benevolent activities in 1986," or something soft and gooey like, "Create an image that reflects our longstanding commitment to excellence and solid financial performance."

• *Strategic Planning:* Now describe the process of reaching that goal, step by step. Strategic thinking is the art of examining all options, judging their relative merits, and then choosing the least bad. Remember that a strategy should be something do-able. "Buy every share of Transcept International until we own it. Then liquidate it," is a very clear strategy. "Do everything we can to improve a whole bunch of things," is not.

• *Delegation:* No large task can be handled responsibly without first being divided into a step-by-step list of specific duties. Map these chores out carefully, then put them in chronological order and assign them. Your role as manager is not to *do* everything, but to make sure everything is done.

• *Implement!:* This is the fun part. No matter how big the beast, once it's rolling, it's nothing more than a hierarchy of tasks. Now your job is to put all the pieces together, as they are presented to you, into the coherent whole you envisioned.

• *Follow-Up:* Never allow a piece of work to disappear into the swamp of no-comment. Find out how you did, not merely to generate kudos (which would certainly do you no harm), but also to reach for negatives. That's part of the learning experience you'll need to do a better job the next time around.

You may thus manage not only projects, but your entire career. In that regard, we all share the same mission: "Live long and prosper." No matter how you choose to get there, active shaping of your fate sure beats flailing around and hoping that success will fall into your pudgy lap. It may, you know. But why not help it along?

Managing Down is the art of getting subordinates to do what you want. Those who can inspire others find themselves at the helm of a happy team that delivers the proverbial 110 percent. For you as boss, their achievements are yours. Nobody cares that you didn't do the work. You managed it. That's all that counts, especially to other managers.

Always keep in mind that people need supervision and control, and appreciate, rather than resent, good direction. Put it forth with finesse, not a trowel. No one sees himself as a bit player in the saga of your life, and a touch of humility often serves you better than the tempered steel of authority.

Whether you bark commands or murmur suggestions, com-municate your desires clearly. Too many managers seem to think their people can soak in nutritive ideas by osmosis, like cells do water. Tell your people what you want. This, of course, means knowing what you want. If you don't, or are still working it out, don't blame them when they fail to read your fuzzy mind. Take the time to meet with them regularly, both one-on-one and in groups. And listen not only to the musical sounds of your own voice, but to what they have to say as well. Nonmanagement people have ideas, too.

Finally, develop and promote your talented staff a little more quickly than they deserve. They will be grateful, and strain to their limits to justify your confidence. Besides, if you don't keep them moving onward and upward, they will eventually find a place that will, and depart in glory, leaving you in the worst possible position as a manager—having to do the scut work yourself.

Managing Up is the art of getting your superiors to do what you want. Those who occupy the aerie are no less in need of good management than those in the lower branches of the corporate tree. In fact, since they're generally more capricious, less conventional, and closer to their neuroses than their subordinates are, their need for direction can be acute. The only real control for senior people, however, often must come from below.

Here are some potent tools to help you shepherd corporate pachyderms in the right direction:

• *Schmoozing:* When, in a foul humor, the executive vice-president needs a jester, a bit of banter may warm him. When the CEO is free-associating, hope it's your ear he bends. Humoring, cajoling, kibitzing, and, more often than not, just plain stroking—all are important arrows in your quiver. And if you get the chance to pour a good business idea into the ear of top management in the process, that's what makes it all worthwhile.

• *Selfless Devotion:* Devoting your ideas and energy to his greater glory is also good. Most top guys are ferociously possessive of the limelight and love those who let them hog it. If that means coming up with a great new product idea, only to sign your boss's name to the proposal, remember that you're not losing an idea, you're building your reputation as a team player where it counts—with the manager of the squad.

• *Honesty, Within Reason:* Good upward management is not the same thing as craven yes-manship, which is neither wise nor dignified. No big guy seeks to be surrounded by a pack of sniveling worms—just a few handpicked ones. So don't be afraid to be firm with authority if you feel you're fighting for its best interests. Of course, there's no reason to go nuts. Develop some sense of when candor is admirable and when it's lethal.

Margin is the difference between the money you spend to manufacture, market, and distribute your product and the money paid by the public to consume it. It's profit, your reason for living, and you want to do your best to make it fat and sassy. Say your plant spends a nickel to make a ten-cent flange rod. That represents a booming margin of 50 percent. Lower the cost of production or raise the price to customers and your margin will increase, which spells added profits to the company and an infinitely expandable budget line for you and your gang.

If, however, you work in a cost center, providing legal skills, public relations counsel, or accounting expertise but, sadly, no income, keep a level eye on expenses of all kinds. You've got to justify your negative impact on margin continually, first by establishing the indispensability of your services, then by running the kind of lean ship that can sail comfortably through the gulf between income and outgo. If you're neither indispensable (watch for those consultants slavering in the wings) nor capable of keeping thin (do you really have to buy those new desktop modems?), you're vulnerable. When times get bad, your operation will be among the first to be cannibalized. Sure, your public boiling will keep the pretax profits warm for a while. But that's marginal comfort indeed.

Marketing is a new name for the world's oldest profession: selling. In early days, a salesman laid a hand on the nearest available product and hawked it. As society got more complicated, however, the haphazard pitch was forced to evolve into a science bristling with complicated tools and theories. And that's how marketing was born.

And just in time. Making people spend money in this age of multiple media and fractious demographics is tough. It's no longer a simple matter of hauling your eggplant to the village common, screaming, "Check it out!" and taking in the *zlotys*. Nowadays, you've got to do research on what kind of people eat eggplantlike material, position your pushcarts in just the right corner of the marketplace, price your product with humility and a touch of daring, advertise it, and hire a bunch of bright and shiny men and women to explain to passersby how good it is, not only fried or parmigiana-ed but in soups and salads as well. Then and only then will you be able to pass some coin back to the farmer.

Today, crack marketeers from august universities play the guys in the long white coats. In ivory towers and test sites in the field, they experiment with direct-response mail, door-to-door sales, telemarketing, advertising, packaging, pricing. Sometimes they hit the right combination and create a revenue monster. Other times, they don't, which, to be fair, is not always their fault: People seldom buy more than one coffin per lifetime, and only when they must.

Make the effort to talk to marketeers, for they make fine friends. This may be more difficult than it sounds, since the average marketeer is about as easy to talk to as a nuclear physicist. His brain is stuffed with arcane terminology—bits of jargon, metaphoric definitions, onomatopoeic buzzwords—all of them needed to explain the towering philosophical structure that must be erected to make sure Americans buy at least forty-seven million dollars' worth of whatever he's marketing this year. Although the first minutes, even hours, with a marketeer may be confusing, heavy with business chat and overly filled with secondhand anecdote, eventually a good old-fashioned salesman is likely to emerge, having been waiting patiently in there all the time for the marketeer to put himself to sleep.

Meetings, when they succeed, create a rosy glow of good-fellowship, an eagerness among all parties to attend subsequent sitdowns, working lunches, informal chats, etc., with the same gonzo group. This sense of mutual self-congratulation lies at the warm and fuzzy heart of every corporate culture, so whether you're giving or taking, make it fun.

Fun in a business context, of course, does not mean putting on a bulbous nose and doing a wacky breakdance on the conference table. In the gray and formal atmosphere of a business meeting, you don't have to be loud to be zippy. You just have to help move things forward in high gear and, when necessary, overdrive.

This is most possible if it's your meeting. Prepare a menu of activities beforehand and take no prisoners when somebody bogs down the works. People hate a windbag at compulsory events, and there are few better ways of infusing a meeting with energy than punishing blahmeisters with polite termination. "We've got a lot of items on the scoreboard, Herm," will do wonders to shut a guy off at the pass. Above all else, make sure to *run* the meet, not simply preside. Be easy and cordial when you can or, if you must, tighten the throttle. They may not love you, but they will respect you in the morning.

If you're just a participant, try to contribute something, if only a witty rejoinder or a trial balloon. If you do nothing but warm a seat, people may think you're an indolent slob who does nothing but respond to other people's agendas. Remember, however, that nobody likes a ham, especially other hams. In high-level gatherings, where Zarathustrian self-images preside, it may be best to speak only when spoken to, unless you, as a fellow megalomaniac, must flex your muscles, too.

Memos should be brief, focused communications, not gassy expostulations of opinion, speculation, and personal aggrandizement. That's what the telephone is for. Your memos—if you would like them to be read—should pertain to one subject, be limited to one page in length, and be written in language a child can enjoy. If you don't want them read—always a fantastic tool in halting action on a hated project—make them good and long. Most of the time, though, you'll want your memos to accomplish something. In that case, arm them with plenty of bullets. This is a bullet: •

Bullets provide the beef, or the illusion of beef. While the pressurized potentate might find a dense paragraph daunting, he won't be able to resist the same data doled out in digestible doses. To wit:

• Never write a memo if a talk will do. In these days of post-Japanese minimalism, less paper is more.

• Never write in anger, which should be expressed in impermanent ways, just in case you're wrong.

• Route your memo to the person who most needs to know, not his superiors or yours. Send copies to all those you want in on the party. And observe the strictest protocol when you order their names. You can't blame folks for keeping an eye on their standings, and complaining when they think you got it wrong.

Finally, always close a memo with an action point. "I look forward to hearing from you," is fine. The onus is now on the other foot, and the memo has done its work.

Men's Room is one of the few secret places men have left. It's a wonderful locale to take a brief meeting with another man, tell a joke for the boys, or otherwise indulge in a little male bondage. In fact, never share a row of stalls with another corporate animal without at least exchanging greetings and a mild meteorological observation, although only a jerk demands a decision on a five-million-dollar project over a urinal. Handwashing is a better time for substantive comment. And a chat in the hallway afterward can be a rare moment of noncorporate conversation.

In short, while you don't want to be caught hanging around the men's room all day, make a virtue out of necessity and use the opportunity to trade a bit of vagrant information and humanity. It's only right. The women are at it with a vengeance in the room across the hall.

Mental Health Day is a holiday you decree for yourself when the prospect of going to work makes you want to puke. As you lie abed on that festive morn, consider:

• *Very few things can't wait until tomorrow:* You'll be surprised how many burning issues can use twenty-four hours of thought. Most meetings, it turns out, are discretionary when your sanity is at stake.

• *They owe it to you:* Unless you have five weeks of vacation per year, you've got a case for a stolen day here or there. In companies that shower their workers with a munificent ten working days per year, three or four mental health days are a right.

• *Nobody really cares:* If you aren't thinking about canceling a presentation for fifty sales trainees, or ducking out on lunch with the chairman, relax. Everybody plays hooky now and then, and in turn forgives those who avail themselves of the universal privilege.

Finally, try not to observe a Mental Health Day on a Friday or a Monday. Both result in long weekends and additional reflexive guilt. Further, a lot happens in most offices on those days, and anyone missing is presumed derelict unless they wheezed and honked around the workplace like a Canada goose the day before, and even then . . .

Mergers happen to the nicest companies, especially lately. Although the word conjures up images of two proud powers joining in equal bliss, it is in effect far closer to a marriage of insects. One spouse, and all its bodily parts, will be eaten as soon as intercourse is done.

Your first move, if you wish to survive being merged, is to evaluate the dress code. Members in good standing of any army are expected to suit up in the required uniform, so take a look at what the new guys are wearing and do your best to blend in. If that means trading your vegetable greens and browns for cool, elemental blues and grays, so be it. If your bold and woolly ties must give way to understated neckwear with a hint of polka dot as subtle as goose bumps, go for the look. The issue is *belonging*, which is exactly what you're trying to continue doing.

Observe other aspects of the new parent's style that will give you a chance to show you're with the program. If they go for a desk as bare as the Kalahari, take a rake to yours, at least for a while. If they eschew formal paper, favoring instead friendly little jottings that leave no trace, join the gang as they manage by walking around. Above all, do your part to make friends with the new guys. This won't be too tough. Most of them will be a lot more convivial than the sad and fearful hutch of enraged rabbits your old friends have become. Sure it's ugly, watching your pals twist in the wind, but keep your face, work harder than you ever have before, and survive, one paranoid day at a time. Nobody said marriage was easy.

Messengers are an evil God's answer to those who desire an orderly universe. They come late. They leave without picking up the right packages. They often find their way to the wrong floor and remain there until given further instructions. Some have even been known to leave their signatures—in spray paint—on the fake walnut of your elevator. If you meet one on the street, he may be in such a hurry to get to the wrong place that he inadvertently runs you over with his bicycle. Unless he just had a joint in the park. In that case he might be driving to the incorrect address more slowly.

Deal not with messengers. It will drive you mad. It is their manager, the dispatcher back at headquarters, who must be closely instructed and held accountable. By beeper or by sheer force of terror, he's the guy who can make sure your packet gets delivered—dry, on time, and in basically one piece.

And if they screw up, don't threaten and stamp your feet— just withhold payment. It's amazing how even the most bizarre messenger service snaps to when calmly strangled with a bottom line.

Moderation in all things is the anthem of American business, which is equally tolerant of vices and virtues, as long as they are displayed without flamboyance. There is, however, one major exception to this rule. Don't let anyone catch you being moderate about your commitment to the company, its product, or its profits. That's like being a little bit patriotic in wartime— damn close to treason. So keep your eating, drinking, gambling, gabbing, and abuse of your expense account under reasonable control. And when the flag is raised and a show of zeal is called for, stand up and holler with the rest of the gang. It's part of being a proud recruit in the army that serves your glorious cause.

Neatness, in nonfascist institutions, doesn't count, as long as you don't harbor rotten fruit in your drawers, allow dead animals on your desk, or lose things. A lot of very competent people need clutter to keep their myriad projects before their eyes. To such as these, filing equals forgetting, and chaos means vitality. This insouciance is all very well and good, until you toss out your paycheck with your lunch. If you're an exploding-office type, thin out the wreckage every now and then, not just for others, but also to keep your own head in shape, at least for a while. And ignore the taunts and clucks of the anal-retentives in your midst, even big ones. They're compulsives, too, with no call to be sanctimonious. Fight for the right to play your kind of game on your kind of terrain. That means maintaining certain standards of your own, even in sloth. The question is not whether the office is in order, but whether the work is. That's where neatness does count.

Nerds will inherit the earth, if they haven't already. Don't be fooled by the superficial trappings of nerdishness—the dweeby eyewear, ill-fitting suits, hair that pokes out at odd angles as if its owner has but recently been aroused from a drunken sleep. Inside every well-placed nerd is a buccaneer, fiercely proud of his abilities, contemptuous of face men, reveling in the gaudy red and blue costume tucked beneath the Clark Kent suit. The fact that smoother operators underestimate him is one of his most powerful weapons. That, and the fact that since childhood, the nerd has been staving off the pokes, giggles, and downright kicks in the ass that the truly socialized have been pleased to offer in the way of friendship. To survive, and achieve, the nerd has had to be tougher, more stubborn, and smarter.

As convivial types have cornered sales and marketing, nerds have conquered the twin redoubts of computer technology and financial analysis. From there, they manage the two prime assets of a company—information and money. When the mega-million-dollar information system goes screaming down in flames with spread sheets, databases, and every word generated in the last ten months trapped forever in its bowels, it will be a nerd who gooses its guts and reclaims the information. When the parent, in July, demands a complete breakdown of the division's ten-year strategic plan for publication in four-color splendor by September 1, bet your credenza a nerd will be in charge. And that's as it should be. Management knows the job will be done with great precision accompanied by the absence of any individual kink.

Networking is very important, yeah, yeah, yeah. If the idea of working someone is not alien to your nature, go thou to lunch with someone who is just as busy working you. You may then tell your friends: "Had a terrific chat with Harry Barber at Universal Implement. He's going to put me in touch with Jane Reever at Brand Cans." This creates the sensation of career growth.

But at what cost? Networking is built upon the ageless assumption that "it's not what you know, it's who you know." This philosophy has always been obnoxious to anyone who believes applied labor to be the best and most honorable route. These tend to see networkers as insincere self-promoters always looking for a leg up. Consider that the prototypical networker of his generation is Jerry Rubin, and realize the limitations of the habit. Excessive networking is also a dead tip-off that you're looking for a job. If you weren't, you'd be in Iowa City talking to your vendors instead of at home in New York working your nets.

So keep in touch with your friends, sure, and watch out for them as they do you. But unless a casual power acquaintance is bound to change your life, save the networking for Larry Tisch.

No is a serious profanity, but sometimes it is the only word that will do. A "no" may establish you as a man of integrity, or peg you as a stooge who won't follow orders. It's up to you. History shows us that sometimes it's wrong to follow orders. But those who don't toe the line even when asked very nicely may soon find themselves charged with insubordination. That's a capital offense just about everywhere. So most of the time, hold your no's and fight the good fight with a little subtlety. Unless you're being told to fly over Toledo and dump some "perfectly harmless" nuclear waste, why get confrontational? Much may be tried before you must utter the two-letter word:

• *Buy Time:* "Gee, Barton, it's a mighty big chunk. Give me a couple of days to see if it's do-able," should suffice. Yes, he may be a little miffed, but that's better than promising something bogus, or impulsively burning a bridge. If the guy is prepared to make your life miserable on the spot, however, it may even be necessary to strike a pose of provisional acceptance, just to get out of the room. Don't feel bad. The battle has just begun.

• *Death by Consensus:* Establish an immediate protocol, via incessant, informational memoing, that everyone involved in the Big Bummer agree on everything. Hold many meetings where nothing is resolved. Most projects—good or bad—will die of a surfeit of critique.

• *Murder by Priority:* You've most certainly got a lot of hot dishes on your plate. If the pressure keeps up, an affable, "I'll get on that right away, Jim, if it's okay for me to shelve the Poindexter deal for a while," should provide some perspective.

• *Passive Resistance:* Simply lying in the middle of the road and doing nothing also works. Sometimes this may be done with silence. Bland agreement followed by inaction can also serve. When it does not, however, the hour you've avoided has come.

• *Say It with Flowers:* Okay, you're too busy, or too nause-ated, or too ethical, to give the guy what he wants. That's no reason to be mean. An honest explanation of your difficulty may have to be offered eventually, as a last resort, larded with as many apologies, excuses, and general explanatory effluvia as you think will put the matter to a civilized end. Convey enough backbone to get the job done, but no more, and make sure to allow the other guy to get away with his self-importance intact. Once his pride becomes the issue, you have lost. So try to make your rejection a bow to his power, not a slap in its face.

Getting turned down by a pro can be a pleasure. Make that "no" a positive experience for you both. You may want the chance to say "yes" next time around, and you're certainly not looking for the opportunity to say "good-bye."

Numbers Cruncher is the guy who smashes a glut of figures through a financial spread sheet and sees what comes out the other end. Spread sheets are designed to calculate the effect one little statistical change will have on the big picture. If you boost planned revenues by 1 percent, what impact will that have on the bottom line? If you increase your debt by 3 per-cent, how does that alter the tax situation? The cruncher feeds one targeted digit into the hopper and watches its effects ripple all the way down the line. These permutations on the basic model are like hothouse flowers, essentially alike yet streaked with one slight color variation. They are called "iterations," as in, "I saw the third iteration on the Tuscaloosa turnaround, Sid, and I'd say you and your team are on to some promising solutions. Keep tinkering."

Crunching numbers, even in this computer age, is meticu-lous, boring, grinding labor, and numbers crunchers are often as delicately wired as the machines they run. How would you feel if you knew the ultimate implications of everything?

O

Obedience is assumed until proven otherwise, so don't prove otherwise. Corporations, like all paramilitary organizations, function according to the odd concept that orders are made to be obeyed, if not without debate, at least without undue sass. This is the active principle behind the holy act of delegation, which is itself the basis of all sound management. Don't mess with it. Those who let it be known they do not blindly obey direct commands are placing their loyalty to their boss—and the corporation of which he or she is an officer—under suspicion. Virtually all forms of nonconformity are tolerated but that.

Best, therefore, to make sure the subject of obedience never arises. It's totally kosher to kick around the wisdom of a particular strategy before you accede to it as a formal order. The ability to offer your view is, in fact, an important aspect of genuine, intelligent obedience. Any boss who doesn't encourage his people to contribute their perspective is bucking for Nazi of the Year award and no fun to work for to boot.

Once the final decision is arrived at, however, you'll have to create the impression that you hear the marching orders and will live by them whether you agree or not. After all, if you wanted freedom, you would have been a street musician. For how to handle those times when a policy makes you so queasy you cannot comply, see **No.**

113

Office is your comfy nest. In its friendly confines, you preside over meetings of your making, inhale a noontime sandwich in relative sanity, catch a snooze on a lazy August afternoon, sign documents that will determine your future, talk to your wife about who's going to pick up the dry cleaning, read, think, live.

Your office is you, sure, but not the real you, not the you that drinks a six-pack when you get home, tears up the bills, and kicks the dog. That "you" should be left where it can enjoy itself. Your office belongs to the guy who shows up with a Danish and a cardboard cup of coffee as close to nine as possible and works pretty much nonstop for the duration. That allows for a wide range of acceptable decor.

Whatever its appearance, use it as a place of power, the one locus in the entire company in which you enjoy a recognized home-court advantage. Don't press it. Just enjoy it. People enter your office to ask for things on your turf, to take instruction, to kibitz over your backyard fence. That's quite different from being summoned elsewhere. You can't put your feet up on someone else's desk.

Office Party is not an occasion to make an ass of yourself, even if that's the way you celebrate the holiday. People are festive, to be sure, even loaded, but that doesn't mean there aren't a few more sober eyes squinting around the room. And drunk or not, folks don't need a full frontal display of your unbridled exuberance in deed or speech. The executive vice-president may never be able to forget the image of you dancing with that side of beef, no matter how hard he tries.

Office Space should not be evaluated by size alone. Other fine criteria include:

• *Location:* Good office space lies in well-traveled avenues, not secluded cornices where valuable drop-in business is unlikely. You don't, on the other hand, want to be directly across from the john, elevator, or coffee machine. If people find you in their face six or seven times a day, they just might start looking the other way. The highest prestige in any building is the corner

office, thanks to the view. It's a great relief to have a nice
window or two to gaze out of now and then, especially when
the meetings grow long and your attention short.

• *The touch that adds so much:* Pictures, plaques, art—
hang it all. Tiny toys for your desk. Banners for your lamp. A
bust of anyone but Karl Marx. Plants, if you can keep them.
Any totem that will help you possess your space. If you're
interested in leather masks, or taxidermy, of course, keep it to
yourself.

• *Hardware:* A computer is now the ultimate window dress-
ing for every office, and it transforms a closet into a worksta-
tion. But don't stop there. If you can get a modem, laser printer,
or any other serious electronic geegaw, you've just transformed
your office into an information center. People will come from
all floors to see your setup, and leave feeling that you're just a
little more of a hot rod than they thought.

• *And then, of course, there's size:* Ultimately, it's all that
really counts. An office is your center of operations, and officers don't work in huts. Watch for vacancies—they do arise—
and militate constantly for room befitting a big guy like you.

On Hold, like any form of psychic abuse, should be accepted as a part of life. A total unwillingness to go on hold,
while certainly admirable, will cut down your telephone intercourse considerably, especially with busy people. The moment
you find your duodenum dancing into knots, however, hang up
and call back later, but only if you want to. If he's the one who's
selling, he had his shot at you and blew it. Why not let him get
in touch with you next time around? Maybe you'll have to put
him on hold for a while. After all, you're busy, too.

For times when heavy hitters put you into a Dantean limbo
you must endure with patience, you'll need the tool no self-
important officer should be without. See **Squawkbox.**

Opportunities are problems in disguise, or is that the
other way around . . . ?

Either way, every challenge that faces you should be seen as
an opportunity, whether it is or not. This is known as the *power*

of positive thinking, and it will help you do better. You will be focused, energized with ambition. This great attitude in turn will create tons of opportunity situations, which you can seize. That's the theory, and loads of people say it has worked for them.

Of course, it's hard to view your secretary's theft of a large bank deposit and subsequent murder by the operator of a small motel as an opportunity. But anything's possible. Maybe you could sell the movie rights.

Paper is forever. All other media pass into forgetfulness, but paper does not, even if the ideas or numbers it contains are dry husks from long-ago campaigns. It is memory.

But who needs to remember everything? Laundry lists of old chores, files from the stone age, newsletters, trade publications, cards that jam your Rolodex until it explodes in your face every time you riffle it—weed these out when they begin to impede your movement. Be ruthless. The file on interactive teleconferencing can go, as can most of the effluvia on your desk. When you find it impossible to cast a particular scrap into oblivion, don't. Maybe it's something to remember.

The trend these days is away from paper. This is because most people don't like to read, except at the beach. It's a lot more fun to pop into another office, shoot the breeze, get a clearance, and while you're at it, whiz through the executive maze for a little power-base interfacing. There's a lot to be said for this approach, and it should not be sneezed at.

However. When the matter is serious, put it in writing, no matter how informally you search for greatness the rest of the time. Good paper helps you generate ideas and, even more important, helps you share those ideas with other people who have brains, who may criticize, get involved, and then take ownership, along with you, of the decision in question. In other words, it covers your ass a whole lot better than a fast word with the chairman at the Xerox machine. More elegantly, too.

Parachute, in both gold and platinum, is the special kind of severance big guys can negotiate for themselves when they are being eased out, not for things they did, but for things they didn't do. Sins of commission are punished. It's the collection of small missteps, the gradual moldering of viability, that leaves a guy so far out on a limb he's practically airborne. How to remove him without a bloody, protracted Götterdämmerung? Offer him two years' pay, a block of stock, and an office and title for six months or a year, or until he finds another job. That ought to do it, if he's sane.

If your former beloved workmates have suddenly turned into a bunch of assassins hacking at your limbs with blunt objects, hang tough and don't quit. Make them fire you and pay for the privilege. You made a contribution, planned a future, bought a midtown condo. Stick it to them. They will pay, and a lot more than you're worth, too, because they are guilty, and scared of their reflection in your fate. And most of all, they'll pay because they expect the same parachute to blossom above their heads when their time is nigh. After you're fired, by the way, resign. It's the polite thing to do, and everyone knows what it means. Guys with a future don't leave due to "philosophical differences." They're too busy jumping ship.

Parent is the organization that owns the organization that owns the one that owns yours. Parents are gray and sober of mien, and they tend to nag a lot. "What are you going to do about your future?" they whine, or "How can you merge with a firm like that?" They scold you when you get into trouble, demand devotion and obedience, and then tell you your life is your own. This parent could also divest you without a tear, cut out your brain and decentralize it throughout the fifty states and Mozambique, or make you travel to Dubuque in the winter. So it pays to make a big fuss when it visits and to tread lightly when you are a guest in its home.

Don't be timid, though. While the parent itself is a monolith, the people that inhabit it thirst for friendship from the field, and to them, that is you. They're easy to work with, too. Parent operations are often like spaceships on a long intergalactic journey, with people and projects in a pleasant state of suspended animation from which they will awake when you are long dead. Working within their deadlines can be bliss. To a genuine Parent person, three months is immediately, and a year is tomorrow.

Performance is your level of professionalism as it is perceived by others. Your opinion doesn't count. Sure, you know you've been operating on all burners since January 1981 with nary a pit stop for rest and refueling, but that makes no difference if the end result of your labors is a gigantic yawn from the body politic.

In short, performance is part reality, part hype. Your goal is to create not only real, solid achievement—that's taken for granted—but also the public acclaim for your amazing industry, competence, and reliability. Modesty is a virtue best shown before those who already know your value.

Perks are what's coming to you, over and above your obscene salary, in recognition of your elevated status and general wonderfulness. See perks as your right, not a guilty indulgence. Extensive perquisites mean the firm is doing well and recognizes your contribution. Company cars, expense account potables and ingestibles, free tickets to the ballgame or ballet—whatever you can get without paying its rightful price is fair game.

Like any status symbol, however, perks are grossly flaunted only by nouveaux arrivés. Those used to the frills that accrue to prowess accept them casually, without fanfare. In front of fellow members of your firm, bacchanalian enjoyment of perks helps destroy the essential impression that you care at least marginally about the bottom line. Conspicuous display in front of clients, too, is crass, for they are the ones who ultimately foot the bill. Be generous, of course, as befits your station, but it's tough to convince a guy you're giving him a terrific price break when you pick him up in a leased Maserati, dine at Chez Oiseaux, and wrap up the evening drinking one-hundred-forty-five-year-old brandy at your personal pied-à-terre overlooking the park, all on company plastic.

Piles, for semi-organized types who cannot change their ways, can be a particularly valuable mechanism to control clutter. Simply keep all current paper in a neat stack at your right hand. Every evening at the close of business, flutter through your pile briefly, placing the stuff that needs action on top and tossing the detritus.

At certain critical junctures, an entire pile may suddenly be superfluous, as once critical projects vaporize into optionality. In that case, instead of eradicating the footprints of the last forty-seven days in one fell swoop, you may take your entire pile, intact, and place it lovingly in the depths of your credenza. Don't worry if that piece of furniture has become totally engorged. You can throw away its entire contents with no regrets when you do your spring cleaning next fall.

Plastic is credit cards. It comes in two varieties, personal and company. This is one of the most engaging false distinctions on record in the world of American business. Plastic is plastic. And it's good.

A personal credit card, for any moron willing to keep good receipts, can function just as nicely as a company credit card on your expense account. Try to get your payback from the boss *before* you venture to handle that whopping American Express tab that arrived after last month's corporate retreat in Sri Lanka. Remember, too, that you can also take what is known as an "advance against expenses" to offset any outlay you may have been forced to make on your personal plastic. Just ask your secretary for details. And enjoy.

A company credit card simply does the same thing, except its use may, in fact, be more closely monitored. Whatever you do, don't try to pick up that jumbo size of Luv's Diapers with your company plastic. If you're big enough to have it, you should be able to keep your right hand informed about what your left hand is buying.

Either way, plastic gives you a wonderful sense of reflected grandeur and affluence and relieves you of the need to carry cash. It's a wonderful perk. Master the possibilities.

Politics is the ability to get your projects moving through a sea of conflicting agendas and outright opposition. To do this, you need other people's support. Folks with good political instincts know how to wield three weapons well:

• *Diplomacy:* Call it insincerity, but those with the gift of defusing opposition with pure cordiality have a supreme leg up over those who try to bull their ideas through on sheer willpower alone. There are few people who will continue to stand in your way if you put a nice schmooze on and refuse to be ruffled. At the very least, your diplomacy will pinpoint where the exact source of their contrariness lies, and what kind of political campaign it will take to turn that negativity into support. Key to this talent is the ability to never get mad, except at one's friends and family.

• *Quid Pro Quo:* Everyone has a price, and unless that price is your skin, it pays to meet it in a little sweet tit-for-tat. The ability to solve problems by appealing to everyone's self-interest is the hallmark of good corporate politics. They call it pragmatism, and it's a big personal plus.

• *Persistence:* The good politician never takes Maybe for an answer, and, ultimately, this stubborn zeal wears down even the most recalcitrant of foes. The fact is, few people care so profoundly about any given business issue that they are impervious to a full-court press that just won't quit.

Finally, remember the limitations of the art, and don't politicize everything you do. Sometimes simple friendship, or a straightforward entreaty, works just as well. Guys who play politics over where they sit at lunch eventually dine only with one another, being simply too smooth and full of subtle agendas for normal human tolerance for more than a couple of hours a year.

Positioning is a buzzword gleaned from the marketing business. It describes the way a product conquers a niche in the marketplace, establishing something unique about itself that can be described, credibly, as a benefit. From this knoll, it can safely attack its competition, which clearly does not possess this wonderful thing. Thus we are given Pepsi, which expresses the soul of a new generation (old people can drink it, too), and Burger King, which has the folks who demand flame-broiled burgers sewn up.

People—the most flexible product of all—can be positioned just as aggressively. If you hear an executive confide, "I'm positioning myself for a major-league run at this," you know he means business. It doesn't matter if he's selling you bran to prevent cancer, the acquisition of a network, or simply himself. He knows where he's coming from.

Power corrupts, and absolute power corrupts absolutely. Big deal. Life without it is Kafkaland. Power gives you the right to tell people to do things, which is okay. It also helps you to stop situations from developing when they could be bad for you personally, and for that reason alone, power is good. Unless you can't manage it. Quite a few people can't. These tend to be egomaniacs with a thin shell of grandiosity, or vice versa. Such guys get bossy, and terrified by the weight of their duties, and eventually go insane. No, they don't wear a hockey mask and gibber down the hallways, but they might as well for all the good they do.

Power, unalloyed with ambivalence or conscience, may also be evil. And although there are certainly evil people around, the vast majority of harm is done by decent people convinced of the absolute correctness of their positions. After all, the human mind can persuade itself that anything is right. Keep your power reined to your humanity by actively consulting with friends, allies, foes, and partners at every stage of the contest. They will socialize your actions, tending to limit the quotient of rampant evil they produce. Unless, of course, you're all a bunch of Nazis.

In the words of the immortal Jock Ewing, power isn't something you're given, it's something you take. But there's no need to be ruthless. In its civilized form, power arises from one of two sources: charm, or good management. If you've got both, congratulations. As for power, use it wisely, but use it. You don't want it to fall off, do you?

Power Base is the amalgam of people you may count on to support you until it becomes inconvenient for them. They are not simply those of great stature or influence, but every person who can share your joys and headaches and still like you well enough. You can't do without them. Nobody, no matter how talented, stubborn, or downright mean he may be, is an island. Every idea moves forward only as it's accepted by others, then promoted as their own, first individually, then in clots. As the power base firms up, so does the general level of acceptance afforded your notions. Eventually, your work will sluice through the infrastructure faster than corn through a goose.

Your power base will also protect you from minor dangers, since you are every bit as important to those in it as they are to you. But don't be fooled into a false sense of bravado by the nearness of your chums. Yes, they are loyal. Yes, they are willing, even eager, to help you along in your quest for the best. But they're not going to fall on a sword for you, any more than you would for them. Such things are only done in friendship.

Prioritizing is creative procrastination. Everything on your blotter at this moment takes up mental space. If they all have equal importance, your mind will be a raging cyclone of notions, schemes, and strategies, all colliding in the whirlwind. This stinks. Prioritizing is the process of deciding which of your duties need to be done *right now, sometime later,* or the festive *maybe next week.* It is made up of the following steps:

• *The List:* Every morning, or at close of business, make up a list of all pending activities. If there are more than twenty or fewer than four, you're in some kind of trouble.

• *Red Ink:* Now strike out the dumb things that aren't really projects at all, just distant threats—housecleaning, dead or dormant ventures, calls you'd rather not, need not, make. You can worry about them over a beer at home.

• *To Do, for Real:* It's easy to get swept up in the little pageant of activities each day represents, and that's fine. Just make sure, while you're playing things loose and responsive, to keep an eye on all those written duties. They're just as important now as they were last night at 5 P.M. when you were tearing your hair out and trying to prioritize them.

• *Do It Again:* Keep it up. If your list doesn't change, you may not be working as efficiently as you think.

Prioritizing is not only a housecleaning tool. It's a sign of how you define, and redefine, your role. Titles remain, but jobs, and their attendant expectations, are living things, continuously in flux. One year you may be chomping on budgets six months at a time. Suddenly you may find yourself traveling with executives as they evaluate assets for sale. The next, you may be lunching with investment analysts and that's about it. Scrutinize your priority list for what has become important, and you'll be ten steps toward managing it.

Private Life is a God-given right for anyone who earns less than $175,000 a year. Above that level, go for whatever time you can grab, sure, but don't expect to see your kids grow up. Most folks, thankfully, are paid the kind of money that leaves them always wanting something. Since you can't have that second home, yacht, or personalized bowling ball, you might as well have time to drink to excess, watch "Love Boat," or fight with your wife. Any company that would deny you a life outside its walls is after something greater than good performance, something, unless you're a budding Faust, you might not be willing to part with just yet.

Procrastination is not a habit, or a strategy, or even a mistake by some poor fool who should know better. It's a way of life, a total approach to doing business practiced by those who need to exist on the edge of destruction in order to do their best.

The procrastinator's is a lonely, scary road indeed. But it's his. And he loves it.

At the same time, procrastinators suffer for their kicks, suffer a lot, suffer when they're working and even when they're not. Like all tragic figures, they are driven by compulsions hoary with psychic resonance and impossible to deny. Those who live with this addiction must still earn money. There are no halfway houses, no hot lines to get them over the rough spots. So pity the procrastinator, as long as he doesn't pull a Hamlet on you and take five acts to do a job that should be executed in one.

Keep in mind that once a procrastinator gets going he is often a super-performer with tremendous energy, intelligence and the ability to move like a greased pig. He has to be, if he's going to live to procrastinate another day—preferably tomorrow.

Profanity is very popular with most executives, who use it to relax and to show they're not *that* square. Know, however, that a healthy percentage of people in corporate life are, indeed, every bit as straitlaced as they appear. Many of these blue-noses have achieved a station they feel is too elevated for anything as immature as swearing, and consider smutty talk an affront to their magnitude. So before you slap a guy on the back and holler, "Larry! How the fuck you doing?" you might want to comb your memory for any concrete proof that the guy's got a mouth on him. Until that's proven, don't talk filth.

And if you're with someone who likes to sling it, don't exceed the general level he's laying down unless you know each other pretty well. There's a big difference between an irregular smattering of hells, damns, or doggones and a fusillade of excretory imagery. And any derivative of the ultimate four-letter word should be reserved for friends and peers alone, even if the chairman is regaling you with stories of his experience at Korean whorehouses. He'll remember the morning after what a profane guy you were.

Profit Center is a part of your company that makes money. It might not plan on how to do it, or evaluate better ways to accumulate it, or invest it afterward, but it does produce it.

Any other function in the organization is a cost center, and it exists solely to primp, prod, and otherwise serve the great money machine. But that doesn't make a profit center the all-powerful entity in the corporation, or afford it the highest regard, nor should it. Some people are breadwinners. Others are homemakers. Both are important, and each needs the other to survive.

So in whatever cornice of the corporation you find yourself, be proud of your function—even if it costs the operation a hundred million dollars a year.

If you are a piece of the revenue engine, however, be aware of your power over the money sponges that hold your hand and monitor your progress. You confer legitimacy on them—professionally and personally—as much as they do upon you. Fact is, if you don't work with them well, chances are they soon won't be working at all.

Promotion is easy, if you rate it and are willing to risk your life to get it. There are times when the 'damn the torpedoes' approach is fully warranted, like when the promotion is so long overdue, or so often promised, that failure to grant it would propel you right out the door. Gonzo-ism often pays off, but you have to be able to back it up with hell-for-leather guts, which means you have to be in war paint to do it right. And you have to be prepared to lose. Are you?

The moderate route, which works just as well and is a lot less dangerous, is even tougher in some ways than risking your neck in one bold plunge. You've got to sink your teeth into the leg of your manager and not let go until it's time to snap up the prize. If you're doing a good job, he'll eventually cave in. Having one of your valued employees incessantly in your face, sighing, accusing you with thorny glances, threatening, cajoling, will, after a time, become intolerable. He'll move mountains to get you humming again.

Begin your drive with a formal request for meeting, which should be scheduled at least a week in advance. No matter how many times you meet informally in the interim, refuse to pinpoint the issue, since this is the easiest way for your boss to dilute or deflect your frontal assault. Let the battle be waged on ground of your choosing. Be evasive, if necessary. You know how. "I'd prefer not to talk about it until then, Marty," should close the matter with all but the most nervous, who, in any event, will now be at your mercy. When the time comes, state your case forcefully, but not belligerently. He will tell you it cannot be done until the waning years of the century. You allow that the whole situation makes you unhappy. Do not resolve the situation. Simply leave, sadly. Then work your ass off, and start a tempest of nagging that does not abate until you win. If you don't succeed within six months, start looking elsewhere. A new job is still the best way to double your income in ten minutes.

Proprietary Information is nobody's business but your own. Revelation of proprietary information is a sin punishable by exile, and rightfully so. A corporation is a very small government, and its state secrets are every bit as vital to its well-being as classified information is to the White House. People who reveal such secrets are called spies.

What is and what is not proprietary may vary widely. In any company, there is a continuous, dynamic struggle going on between those who want to disclose basic data about the firm, and those who want to play things close. Both sides are right. A company needs to keep a stream of information going outward in order to appear financially sound and attract the interest of analysts. On the other hand, you don't owe the outside world a goddamn thing except an annual report (and not even that if you're privately owned), and there had better be a sound business reason to spill your guts. Somewhere in the middle of these positions is sound policy on proprietary decisions. You've got to have a very clear picture of what facts are to be made public, in writing, if necessary. And if, when pumped, you have any questions or doubts, refer the matter to the department responsible for protecting the gates. For a discussion, see **Public Relations.**

Public Relations is also known as Public Affairs, and Corporate Affairs, and sometimes even Corporate Communications. Whatever it calls itself, it's all PR. It's a shame this profession hasn't got the sense to call itself by its proper name—public relations—for it fulfills a crucial and dangerous function. Public relations is the face of the corporation, complete with ears, eyes, a nose, and, mostly, a mouth. In a company in good control, that face—not the heart, brain, or spleen—does the talking. That position as spokesvoice gives PR the need to know a wide variety of material, and to help decide which of it is proprietary, in short, to set public policy. This is very great power indeed, and PR people sometimes rise to the highest advisory roles. They do not, however, grow up to be king. For that, you have to be able to read a spread sheet, and most public relations people, honestly, would rather not.

Public relations employees write speeches, news releases and statements for public distribution, produce videotapes and media plans that manipulate the fourth estate quite effectively, make decisions on corporate contributions, handle customer complaints, and do basically anything else people want. The job also has the power to make you famous, if you like to talk to trade publications.

In general, the profession breaks down into three types, each of which must be managed differently:

• *Institutional:* These guys know their function and don't mess around. They don't leak information, they rarely get into a schmoozing frenzy, and they're a little gray around the edges. They work best with people who make reasonable demands and give them a due date. They tend to believe in the company and its mythology, since that is their lifeblood. After work, they turn plaid and tell anecdotes.

• *Showbiz:* The prototypical PR person is a cross between a first-class pitchman and your aunt Minnie—seeping information and gossip about mutual acquaintances like wet cheesecloth, schtupping food, plying you with drinks, whining, pleading, giving you hockey tickets, all to get you to do what he wants. This may vary. If you're with the media, he may simply want you to publicize the movie star or shoe company that he represents. If you're a friend in the corporation, he may be seeking the right to sculpt a campaign that will make you a famous person in the industry trade papers. Whatever it is, he's up to something, and it could do you good. Just because he takes excellent lunch doesn't mean he can deliver, though. Make him back up his chat with performance.

• *Rogue Elephant:* Every now and then, after years of incessant conviviality, a PR person goes berserk and begins revealing in his everyday communications a mixture of weariness, cynicism, and impatience with every kind of cant. Obviously, such guys should be given a wide berth. They carry the seeds of their own destruction, and know it, and wish to spread it just as an apostle of some new idea trumpets the truth. Nothing is more dangerous to a culture than the man who has heard the terrible, yea, existential news. For some reason, a life in public relations seems to impart that message.

Quality means something that works for a year without breaking. To provide this towering level of customer satisfaction, companies must rouse workers out of a reasonable, profound alienation from their labor into a state of personal dedication. This oneness with the goals and values of the company produces quality and, not coincidentally, revenue.

There are two ways of producing euphoric corporate patriotism in normally canny people: more money, or brainwashing. The latter is cheaper. Enter the quality industry, led by visionaries who teach you how to achieve it without tears, and for free. The fact that error-free performance from workers does not require higher wages is, naturally, a powerful lure to the guys who sign the checks.

The good news for American consumers is that the quality propaganda process, as outlined by a variety of pop stars from Crosby to Peters, works. Give people a strong anthem, decent but not generous wages, a common enemy (the Japanese, Burger King), and a forum to share their ideas and success stories, and they will begin to deliver quality performance. Give toys to those who publicly deliver quality. Pins, ribbons, calculators, a night at Denny's, whatever will be interpreted as a pat on the back, not a bribe.

A word of caution: this process demands total sincerity from general management, and the financial investment, when necessary, to make sure people have the tools to do their jobs right. At the first whiff of cynicism from the top, the troops will be sickened, and turn sour on you, probably forever, resulting in the level of performance you deserve. So once you begin talking quality to your own folks and not just customers, beware. You may have to put your money where your mouth was.

R

Reporting Structure is the branch of the corporate tree on which you sit. Below you on your bough, hopefully, there is a thick foliage of smaller limbs, sprigs, and shoots that you can shake around. Above you, probably, there are the tender leaves of senior management that move you when they rustle. Although your career is spent in your reporting structure (with a thin tendril to another branch here and there), never fail to notice and serve the total tree, from the solid trunk of salespeople or factory workers on up, and outward. As the twig is bent, so goes . . .

Responsibility for most things should be shared, like Chiclets. This is not only sensible, but just. Most actions taken by your company are not the by-product of your lone personal whim but the result of a complex interlocking consensus. To take the heat by yourself for actions only partially within your purview is bad and dangerous policy.

Responsibility may best be distributed throughout your organization via paper. Memo a variety of players when you've got a key notion on tap, and "cc" those who should know what's on. This will spare you any claims of ignorance from your fellow professionals when responsibility for an unsuccessful strategy curdles into blame. The flip side of this careful approach, however, is that *credit* must also be shared. While the glutton for praise in all of us may find this *politesse* a little hard to stomach, mutual kudos engender a sense of common accomplishment that does wonders in cementing your power base. That's worth a lot more than a kiss on the cheek from top management.

As with any good thing, of course, it's possible to carry healthy consensus too far. When responsibility is spread overly thin, decision-making grinds to a halt. In departmental matters especially, the senior manager must ultimately bear the burden for the plans and actions of his squad, since that is the essence of his charter. Don't let the desire to communicate decay into gutlessness. Those who seek a comfortable level of power learn to tell the difference.

Restaurant is neutral territory and a good place to open and maintain the kind of friendly relations that presage or arise from success. It is a good place to broach plans and indulge whimsies, and to share a celebratory glass after the battle has been waged and won. It is not suited to substantive negotiations or high-torque presentations, any more than a conference room is the best locale for slam dancing.

Choose your restaurants with an eye toward the tastes and proclivities of your companion, and the kind of agenda you have in mind. If you're dining with a cigar-chomping nabob, you probably won't want to select a *cuisine minceur* emporium featuring plates as large as championship Frisbees which hold only microscopic shards of underdone veggies. If your companion is known to jog ten miles a day and radiates an aura of meat-free health, don't drag him to a beef joint. And don't automatically go for the highest-ticket establishment, either, unless you're trying to impress. Comfort and conviviality at the table is more important than crystal and fresh orchids any day.

Résumé is either totally unnecessary, or slightly so. Either way, it's an overvalued tool. Most of the time, you'll have no use for it whatsoever. You are, presumably, happy at your job, with no great desire to meet a new bunch of oddballs, having grown used to your own. When headhunters call, they generally can be satisfied sans résumé. They want to know you, not your paper, and any curricula vitae can be dispensed over the phone or in person. Don't worry, they'll be taking notes. Lack of a prepared résumé, too, bespeaks your satisfaction with your job, always an enticement to those who seek to move you.

When the sky gets dark and your reign is coming to an end, you may need to assemble a résumé. Don't believe, however, that this document, no matter how superbly laid out and printed, will get you any job but one you don't want. A résumé, at best, is a door opener, and not a very good one at that. Your best friend, mother, or former guidance counselor will do just as well, as will a direct phone call. Once you have your foot jammed over the sill, your résumé is even more superfluous, since success will now ride on your personal sales skills.

So don't lade up your résumé with a load of butterfat. Keep it to one page, be very clear about your past and present duties, and don't be clever. Jokey or creative résumés get an appreciative laugh just before they are consigned to the circular file. Also omit any pompous aeration about your career goals, life objectives, and beloved hobbies. Nobody cares, and it shows you're simply trying too hard to impress. Save your prospective employers the information that you're "Looking for a fulfilling position in account management in which my abundant skills and talents will be actualized." They know that. Why else would you be sitting across their desktop, smiling so hard your face hurts?

Retirement is an affliction that should be contemplated only by those prepared to confront their mortality. It is possible, however, to leave and pursue other interests on the way to your next assignment, if you've got the money to do it. First-class spending is a full-time job, and one of exceeding interest if you've worked for it. Unfortunately, ten minutes after you retire, you will become interested in cruising the malls for the early-bird specials. You will be old, no matter how sharp you look in your new lime greens, and what good is all your money then? Work till you drop.

Revenge is rare. Most of the time you have to wait patiently for a hated enemy to eat dirt, and his demise has little to do with your efforts, underhanded as they may have been. That doesn't mean it wasn't worth a try, and every little bit helps. Corporate revenge must be infinitely surreptitious. The slightest hint of open warfare is odious to the statists who run the empire, as well as to everyone else in an unstable craft not represented by a strong labor union. So plan to savor your campaign, for it's likely to be a long one, with battles joined and abandoned, false peaces, backroom smokes with allies plotting imbroglios, open firefights before the throne, secret poisonings in the board room, victory toasts over midnight bonfires. And through it all, you smile. Good luck.

Rules are mostly unspoken in self-respecting business organizations, but conformance to those unwritten norms is as vital as those pertaining to the reporting of outside income. These subterranean regulations usually involve matters of appearance, lengths of meetings and memos, working hours (actual), amount of travel, manner of address (Marty, Mr. Nagle, sir), and level of acceptable profanity. The mores of your culture are expressed in such details, and you flout them at your peril.

S

Salary is what you fight for. Demand a performance review every six months and you'll see one every nine. Do not believe anyone who tells you what cannot be done. Do not listen to excuses about personnel, its percentages and its bylaws. Demand parity with your functional equals. In short, let your boss or bosses know that you expect to be well paid. They may be annoyed by you, but more often than you would expect or they would like, they'll bump you up. They understand you all too well, and in their hearts, they sympathize mightily. They like money, too.

Sales may be defined as the activity of making another person buy something he didn't know he wanted. After all, if he needed your product in the first place, he probably would have gone out that morning and chased the truck that was carrying it.

There are many methods that promise to teach you how to sell. That's because it can't be taught. How to sell *better,* yes, but the basic talent has to be there or you might as well go fishing—you wouldn't be able to sell a weapons system to a Republican. Selling is an innate ability born of unconscionable self-confidence, a swagger that assumes that, sooner or later, you will fall. And you will, eventually, if he's good. Later, you may ask yourself why, but the specific reason doesn't matter. You were sold, that's all. Now use that digital tomato poacher in the best of health.

If you've got the gift, go about the business of training yourself with a vengeance. America is a nation of salespeople. You're going to have to approach it scientifically if you expect to compete and win. Some tips:

• *Convince Yourself First:* You can't sell something you don't love, so search until you find it. You'll be wasting your time if you don't, because you'll be lousy at selling it. If you notice yourself yapping about the product at such length that your friends tell you to stop, that's a good indication you've stumbled on your mission.

• *Prepare and Forget:* Sure, you've got to have a developed sales pitch, but don't think it's more than a crutch to get you started. Excellent sales is based on spontaneity, and the feeling, in the customer, that he is being treated as an individual, that his needs are being considered, and met, by the product, or, more accurately, by you. It's hard to convince a guy he's very special when you're cribbing off index cards.

• *Full-Court Press:* You've got to let the client know you want his business *badly,* so be prepared to do a bit of discreet groveling. You'll need all your charm and powers of schmooze to make the extra effort fun, not nauseatingly servile. And don't be afraid to brandish theater tickets, golf clubs, free dinners, etc., to get the other guy on your side. Sure, it's crass. But in sales, it's the oily bird that gets the worm.

• *Close It:* Only amateurs talk about the one that got away. The ability to cement the sale is what distinguishes successful pros from future custodial engineers. So don't sit there like a schlub. Ask for the order.

The career is not for everyone. Failure is bleak and terrifying, a gaze into the essential alienation of existence. Success, on the other hand, is sudden and almost sexually gratifying. If you don't get a charge out of close customer contact, yet still have a yen to mold human opinion, why not explore a more civilized line of work—like marketing?

Salespeople tend to be ridiculously positive, talkative to a fault, loyal to their friends, and if you steer them carefully away from their pitch into tales of their hobbies, families, and past conquests on the road, interesting. Hanging around with salespeople, especially after extended sessions with brain-trustees, can be invigorating, for they are unencumbered by excessive ambiguities and self-doubts. This releases you from the obligation to entertain your existential uncertainties, at least for a while. Salespeople go down best when slightly pickled, when their natural bonhomie emerges with no cloying undertaste.

Never let the subtleties of high-level decisionry, and the walking think tanks in gray and blue who people its upper-middle management, blind you to the fact that the bold crudities in sales are the ones who actually hold the mainspring of the business in their hands. Sales is revenue is profit. No profit means new senior management. This is a fact that does not go unnoticed by corporate planners when they're in the market for a chief operating officer. More than one pitchman has grown up to be president.

Satisfaction should come with any job, but don't count on basking in it every day. Weeks may go by, in fact, which are nothing but cosmic grit. If no sun shines for more than a couple of months, however, maybe you'd better start searching for something that will make you happy. You only live once, if that.

Screwing Up is an integral part of the human condition, so don't eviscerate yourself when something punctures, and don't be a prig about it. Apologize and move to correct your error personally. Most folks, painfully aware of their own mortality, expect no more. Those who would seek to humiliate or seriously wound you for a mild indiscretion, however, should be countered with speed and belligerence. They want to do more than educate you. They want to teach you a lesson. Let them know you're a very poor student on such serious subjects. "Sorry about that, Larry, but if you look at the forty other projects on my plate, I think you'll see the rest of my output is up to snuff," should let an assailant know you don't intend to be trussed and broiled. If he doesn't go away, mount some counter-surveillance and wait. He'll get his.

A multitude of minor screw-ups, on the other hand, is as bad as a major fuck-up. Worse, in fact. After you've spilled plutonium for the fourteenth time, people will find it hard to believe you won't do it again.

Secretary is the noncommissioned officer who gets things done, the best conduit of corporate information about every subject from new lunch spots to about-to-be-former vice-presidents, the point of entry into any department or executive ear, the keeper of the budget, and the most exploited worm in the ointment. A good one is hard to find, and a bad one is even harder to get rid of. They endure like tugboats while small luxury craft come and go with the tide. Cultivate them all, not just your own. Their friendship makes your life easier, and their general enmity invariably presages disaster. There is no quicker way to general disrepute than to get on the secretarial blacklist, since they talk to each other, and to their bosses, most copiously. And if push came to shove, most guys would take their secretary's word over yours any day of the week. When was the last time you saved his tail by working late?

Fortunately for the payroll, secretaries receive their actual wages—the payment that brings them to the job day after pressurized, nitpicking, semihumiliating day—not in dollars, but in the intimacy they enjoy with power. This proximity creates personality distortions in some executive secretaries, who come to view themselves as a cross between a Jewish mother and Rasputin. Never allow a rampaging secretary to define your relationship with her boss. A firm approach works best. They were born to serve, not command.

See Me, usually scribbled on a memo, letter, or bill, is bad news. Never just pick up the terse invitation and hotfoot it into the boss's office. The phrase actually means: "I don't know what to make of this. Collect your thoughts and let's talk." This is not necessarily offensive, so remain calm. But do go through the relevant correspondence, review your rationale on the mat-

ter, and take a few minutes to look at the ceiling. Then go in and
see him.

If, however, the message is underscored twice, or seasoned
with an exclamation point, make your cogitation short and,
once you've determined your actions righteous, sail into battle
with wind in your sails. When you're fifty thousand dollars over
budget on a ten-thousand-dollar project, of course, it might be
wise to go into the inquisition with hat in hand. Cheer up.
Things could be worse. At least the note didn't say "You're
fired."

Sex between peers, as long as you're not persistently dis-
covered *in flagrante delicto* in the computer closet, is just
another time-honored permutation of life in the workplace.
Within a given culture, who plays and who does not is generally
common knowledge. Business is simply too rife with opportunity—from conventions in exotic locales to late-night trysts in
shadowy conference rooms—for the weak of mettle or strong
of gland to resist an escalating amount of clandestine ecstasy.
And after a while, a guy gets a name for himself. This human
failing, in both married and single offenders, is accepted much
like any other: smoking, drinking to excess, voting Democrat,
anything deemed eccentric but not dangerous.

Those committed to a life of dalliance, as opposed to the
occasional lapse, often find it best to stick to people outside
their company, not fellow toilers in the same corporate vineyard. That tawdry episode you enjoyed at the managers' meeting in Omaha last year with the vice-president of strategic
planning casts a weird shadow when the woman is suddenly
assigned to evaluate your profit plan. A reputation for sleeping
your way to greater power, too, is always deeply resented by
those of your peers who perform on their feet, not on their
backs.

The only unforgivable, not to mention illegal, sexual act is
the misuse of your official power to leverage someone off their
feet.

Sexual Harassment, on the other hand, is a sin punishable by firing and, in its most egregious form, by jail. Whichever scares you most, keep it in mind as you regard your secretary, or your assistant, or that vendor from Reno, with lust in your heart. If the person is dependent on your goodwill for his or her livelihood, make certain that any attentions you offer are perceived to be wholly and totally personal, not professional, and any response 100 percent voluntary. This may be tough, because, in all honesty, they're probably not.

If you've gotten to the point of jumping your subordinates, it may be too late for you already. You're out of control. Try to remember, if the unethical aspects of the act only make it more tantalizing, that schtupping people against their will generally makes them want to kill you. And they will, too, when they get mad enough, especially in these days when women seem more inclined to report such crimes, and authorities to prosecute. All it will take is one furious phone call to the chairman to start the wheels of your destruction in motion. Not a squeeze in the world is worth that, unless you're very hard up indeed.

Sleaze Factor is alive and well in most large business organizations, not to mention virtually every level of government. Every big enterprise has its institutionalized nightmare alleys: the chemical plants that boiled over in Bhopal or West Virginia; ten thousand poor folk in the hills of Pennsylvania who have to eat cardboard on Christmas because your firm moved its transponder division to Korea; the quiet subsidiary developing poisonous strands of DNA.

You, of course, work in the breakfast foods division and feel just terrible about the whole thing.

Then there are the not-so-legitimate forms of corporate malfeasance—the bribes that must be offered to some potentate's golfing buddy if you want that big hydroelectric project in that Eastern kingdom. The $469.22 your defense subsidiary charges the federal government for every bobby pin. Stuff like that.

Whether it's legal and simply immoral, or illegal and unethical, too, it's still sleaze. And you don't want any part of it. You're a good person, after all.

The fact, however, is that you, your wife, and your sixteen towheaded little shavers have to live at a certain minimal level of bourgeois comfort. So all you can do is the best you can.

Business organizations are no more intrinsically moral than the rest of the world you have to live in. Unless you are personally asked to murder a German businessman at a dinner theater, don't be more squeamish about your livelihood than other reasonable peers are about theirs. It comes off a little sanctimonious.

Stay clean. Work with like-minded people to minimize the power and influence of the sleaze-meisters. And, like Hippocrates, do no harm.

If your company finances the overthrow and murder of assorted heads of state, of course, you might want to think about jumping ship, or even blowing the whistle. Acceptance of that level of sleaze has a way of twisting you a little out of shape. Permanently. You don't want to become the kind of person your parents warned you against.

Spread Sheet, see Numbers Cruncher.

Squawkbox is the attachment, also known as a speakerphone, that enables you to hang up the receiver and conduct your conversation over the air, broadcasting it for all in your office to hear. This, first of all, frees your hands to doodle, sketch, and take notes, and liberates your poor ear from the overheated plastic that is its destiny. It also renders possible the public conference call, a primary tool of consensual management. Open conference calls are particularly useful when you and your staff don't have the time, money, or inclination to trek all the way to Seattle, or Istanbul, for a little essential consultation with another gang of suspects. The squawkbox is also a lifesaver when you are placed on hold by someone you can't disconnect with impunity. Simply put the offending dead air or Muzak on the speakerphone, and when the party finally appears you'll be ready to chat. Until then, you can go about your business unchained from the instrument of torture.

Like any good tool, this gizmo has its limitations, ignorance of which may be perceived as abuse. Avoid putting someone on the squawkbox without informing them of your decision. "I've got Betty, Barry, and Ted in the room here, Bud, and I'm going to put you on the box so you can share your thoughts with them," should meet with no resistance. Too, never handle any personal call over the open airwaves, unless you're trying very hard to be obnoxious. The quality of human speech over a squawkbox is diminished, distanced, and unfit for informal conversation, and friends and family like to think their phone time with you has some private content. If you try to squawk them, don't be surprised when they holler, "Get me off this thing!" Do so immediately, lest they free their own hands in a less technological way—by hanging up.

Strategic Plan is the formal statement of how the business will be run for a designated period of time. It includes a statement of mission (usually something like, "Do very well for the next six years"), a situation analysis ("Hog snouts will wither in the next twenty-four months under competition from reconstituted beef by-products"), a layout of strategic alternatives ("Get out of pork or corner the market"), and finally, some generic directions the strategic planners feel comfortable with ("Make selected divestitures and acquisitions to enhance the value of our investment portfolio"—and who could argue with that?).

The strategic plan is a very comforting document, and valuable, too, if only for the discussion it generates. But it's bushwah, and the moment the ink is dry it's out of date. The essentials of a business change from moment to moment, and you often can't even plan what you're going to have for lunch tomorrow, let alone which asset you're going to want to pump up or strip down two years hence. It's yet another part of the appearance of scientific certainty that companies like to spin around themselves, the myth that everything is in control, that a large company is not, in fact, a juggernaut hurtling toward an inexorable fate. As such, the strategic plan makes fine reading. But if you really want to know what's going to occur down the road, take a look at the twelve-month financial forecast. Numbers speak louder than words.

Style is the way you, and no one else, do the things you do. It should be a fine blend of personal signature and conformity to prevailing norms. If either aspect goes out of whack—in wild flamboyance or egregious blandness—you will be projecting not style at all, but ego.

Costume makes the most crucial statement about your ability to express personality in the gray zone. Don't confuse style with gratuitous oddity, though. Tartan socks beneath serge slacks, for instance, may be a fine touch as long as your crease stays sharp, but kilts will raise an eyebrow everywhere but Scotland, no matter how nicely you keep your pleats. Conversely, an overly conservative approach may target you as a guy who does nothing but play things safe. In youthful firms peopled by children of the sixties, that conservative reputation can carry with it a "no guts" price tag that does you no justice.

In the particulars of your work, too, keep hovering within the steady confines of culture-specific behavior. If your company likes to do things up close and personal, for example, with a minimum of weighty paper, keep that stricture in mind as you churn out another keester-covering ream of documentation. Keep on writing, though, if that's part of your style—the way you function best. In fact, a good sense of who you are can help to keep you from getting sucked into every inane fad that whiffles through your culture. The key is to speak the same tongue as everyone else, but with your own faint and classy accent, one that bespeaks your background, your breeding, your humanity. The latter is a quality that's never out of style.

Success for the genuinely ambitious is never quite attained, only glimpsed. Like a trek up the Himalayan peaks, each new height attained must be viewed as a staging ground for the next assault on perpetually distant summits only the blessed ever live to see.

Within the breast of every competitor rests a tiny kernel of dissatisfaction, a desire to do more, make more money, wield more power. When that nut is cracked, and an overabundance of self-satisfaction germinates, the drive to excel dies. So earn plenty, and set aside time enough to spend your wages during this lifetime. Grow your reporting structure until your influence spreads outward and upward. In short, live fully the success you have achieved. But don't get satisfied, not ever. The race is won not by the smug, but by the guys fleeing the fierce, hot wind of their own aspirations.

Sucking Up, see **Ass-Kissing.**

Suggestion, as in "the power of," is often the best means of touching the hearts and minds of your countrymen. In an atmosphere where ideas are power, most people like to believe they think up most stuff all by themselves. Your sideways approach allows the other guy to ingest your notion, chew it over for a while, then spit it out in slightly different form as his own. You may then compliment him on the brilliance of his contribution, and have lunch. Now isn't that better than all that squabbling?

T

Team is anyone you're working with at the moment, anyone you're likely to work with, anyone who works with them. The bigger the team, the more guys you can call on to go to bat for your side. In the largest sense, your entire company is a team, but it's tough to think that way when you're deep into body work on the fellow officer who punched you in the teeth on the La Jolla pilot. The only truly important team, fortunately, is the tiny tandem you create when you work well with one other person. For that, you must become the model of corporate success, the team player.

Team Player is what you want to be, and the key to a successful and rewarding corporate life. There are many reasons for failure on the job: stupidity, dishonesty, lack of training, despondency, laziness. Yet the one most often cited as sufficient cause for a guy's career meltdown is: "Jack didn't fit in here. He wasn't a team player." This, in itself, is viewed as a universally accepted provocation for dismissal.

Team playing isn't tough. You don't even have to sacrifice any entrenched positions, not often, since most of your stances aren't all that deeply felt, anyway. All you have to do is listen to each person as if his or her opinion was worth the three minutes it took to deliver. Agreement isn't necessary, although persistent opposition to everything does get on people's nerves. Just work to create the impression that you identify and sympathize with everyone else until proven otherwise.

In certain close cases, where common effort is the only thing that will get business done, you need to offer more than superficial evidence. You need the charge of electric motivation provided by the real thing, team spirit.

Team Spirit is patriotism, the many different breasts that swell as one when a conference ends with the corporate song. It is something larger than yourself, and its true beauty is not expressed in conviviality, or political machinations, or in jolly macho bars, but in *working together.* Playing well as one unit, providing a key product or service to a needy nation, raking in humongous mounds of dough for the master you serve and feed on, all this intense mutual activity creates a rush of naïve fervor, that fuses one and all to the same ideal—Company.

In its malevolent form, team spirit is invoked as the idol to which men and women are expected to sacrifice their families, their introspective selves, their stomach linings. That's not team spirit, that's religion, and a crude one, too.

Telephone is the most wonderful instrument in the world. It obviates the need for in-person meetings with unnecessary people, enables you to touch down on myriad flowers near and far afield, and cuts down on paper flow with direct communication that serves almost as well. There are several simple rules that will enable you to give consistently good phone:

• *Answer Your Own:* The more pompous the poohbah, the harder it is to get him on the line. Of course, your secretary will pick up when you haven't got the time or hand free. But make a practice of being immediately accessible. You'll be rewarded with more friendly voices from beyond.

• *First Impression:* Answer with your name, that's all. "Omnicrude Industries, Department of Mercenary Services, Zack Rambo speaking," is pompous. Folks want to speak with you, not your résumé.

• *No Holding, Please:* Don't leave a guy in limbo for more than a couple of seconds, not unless he tells you he's ready to cop a few z's while he waits for your attentions. The rudest habit of all, no question, is to have your secretary call someone, then place the guy, who did not initiate the contact, on hold. If that happens to you, hang up, if you can. If the king is on the other end of the wire, of course, hang in there. It's more important to wait for him than to work for somebody else.

• *Make It Good:* Unless it's purely a personal call, get to the point and stay there. Ninety percent of a good phone is energy, the feeling that two parties are really communicating in spite of the electronic barrier between them. So reach out and . . . well, you know.

• *Comfort Station:* Above all, make it easy. Put your feet up on your desk, or stand, or pace, or lie on the floor. That's the luxury of being invisible.

Thank You would be nice. Of course, nobody's going to kill you if you don't say or jot it, especially to underlings, but relatively indiscriminate thanking will make folks like you, enjoy working with and for you, and position you as a mighty nice guy who pays his debts. A consistent thanker may also find himself thanked profusely at every turn by grateful thankees of all rank. So don't be constipated with your appreciation. Get it out.

Time is not money. Money is money. If you don't have time to spend it, of course, money is useless, a fact brought home to corporate executives when their plans for the weekend are canceled yet again. Next to money, though, time is of the essence. Important people in particular are impressed with the value of their time, and wasting it is one of the ultimate crimes. Allow the following for each function you're likely to encounter:

• *Chairman:* In one-on-one conversations, complete your business in five minutes. At his salary, anything more is exploitation of a commodity worth more per day than your apartment.

- *Other Senior Officers:* Fifteen minutes, unless he throws you out. Yes, he's busy, but he's only human. Maybe he'd like to have a chat.
- *Vice-Presidents:* Don't worry about it. Vice-presidents have unlimited time to indulge in scheming, planning, gossiping, nagging, politicking, and grousing. In the process, they may get some work done, too. It doesn't hurt to be around in case that happens.
- *Directors, Managers, and Other Professionals:* Five minutes, unless he invites you in and puts his feet up on his desk. The guy is probably taking orders from seventeen higher-ups. Give him a break.
- *Secretaries:* If they're typing or on the phone, leave them alone. If they're not, pull up a chair and prepare to set a spell. They can talk.

Title, like salary, must be won. Even if your wages are increasing apace, which is encouraging, make sure to press for a new title every two years or so. You might not get it, but no one will blame you for asking if your work is exemplary. You may move from manager to director, to executive director, to junior vice-president, to whatever they choose, before you actually gain entry to the vice-presidents' club. Once you arrive there, you'll probably have to make do with money for a while. Attaining a title above that rank means you're not a kid anymore. And there's plenty of time to do that.

Travel is a rigorous demand heaped upon headquarters people by workaholic senior managers who never see home and like that fine. The prevailing decentralization mania that has recently seized monolithic corporations assumes that the executive office exists solely to serve the boonies, that all just power derives from those lusty, simple peons in the field. In addition to encouraging the macho, travelin' man life-style, this philosophy is convenient for budgeteers, since a lean management-on-the-move sure beats in-place staff you have to pay. Thus we see able leaders, in full command of a number of working telephones, consistently yanked from the comfort of

their metropolitan digs and thrust into the cold reality of places
you can only reach by biplane. The only acceptable proof that
you are actually working in such lunatic establishments is to
disappear just about forever from the place in which you were
hired to work, and where you work the best.

Unless, of course, you're happiest on the road. It does have
its rewards. Plastic at every meal. Mucho drinks at any and all
hours. Nice hotels with tiny bars of soap. Miles of smiles from
dawn to dusk until your little face aches from the relentless
jollity. And, above all, the constant illusion of momentum, the
frenzy of planes and limos and taxis and meetings that must
mean progress, the assumption by management that, since they
haven't seen you for six weeks, you must be doing something
very important indeed. Big travel schedules can serve bril-
liantly as a masquerade for a totally fictional function. And be
lots of fun, too.

But if you're serious about your role as corporate animal, do
not lose touch with your roots. You've got politics to nurture,
projects to shepherd, and family to enjoy and aggravate, and
you can't do that on the road. If they wanted a guy with holes in
his shoes, they should have hired Willy Loman. And hopefully,
that's not you.

Turf is the work you do that no one but you should be doing.
Turf should be protected with as much violence as you need,
but no more. Only the paranoid jump at shadows. A straightforward manner is better than foaming at the mouth. "Gosh,
Doug, negotiating third-party leases with independent con-
tractors is my job, I think," will disarm almost any skulldugger
who seeks to snitch what's rightfully yours.

And remember the golden rule. Guys who snipe at other
people's turf have little right to grieve when theirs gets attacked
from the rear.

Union is anathema to the keepers of the capitalist flame. Not that there isn't copious benevolence at the highest levels of the corporate tree toward the average working person and his or her simple, bucolic life. Management looks up to its work force much the way Rousseau admired the noble savage, having no real desire to meet him. "Fancy Farm folks are the best in the world," you will hear executives say, and they mean it, too. Like any parents, they do love their little children. When they're good.

But when they're bad, look out. The prospect of workers getting together to control the terms of their own employment curdles that warm regard into contempt and fear—contempt for the uppity squirts who think they're calling the shots all of a sudden, and fear of the power the whelps possess to strip their masters of the privilege to fire at will.

In secret confab, top management plots to destroy labor unions, decertify them, fire organizers, whatever it takes short of murder to protect their charges' right to work without representation. In short, it's still war, even though Pinkertons are no longer called in to bop heads and chauffeur scabs through picket lines. Which side are you on?

Upside is all the good things that come of a bad action. When your division is relocating to a small township in Asia, think of the opportunities for travel, the tasty indigenous food, the lively local music, and cheer up. The fact that the roads are unpaved, that there is no television, and that women are seen as the source of all evil, well, every cloud has its downside.

Vacation is easier said than done. There's always one heavy hitter who thinks it's funny, after having been prepared for your departure for months, to lean back in his recliner the day before you're set to make your escape, and muse, "Well, well, Gene, you're really planning to go away during the big Fall Promotion. I guess that's loyalty for you." Sure, you'd be justified in punching the guy in the cheek, but to what effect? Just reiterate your plans, describing them with some enthusiasm, if you wish. If he sees fit to cast further witty barbs, feel free to chuckle and nod like an idiot, or for that matter, to sit in silence. Under no circumstance fall into serious discourse on the central issue of whether you are actually taking the trip you have planned with your lover, friends, or family for nearly six months in increasing excitement.

If he pushes beyond false jocularity into veiled threat, you may say, calmly, "I'm taking my vacation, Ted. Unless you want me to check into a mental institution." This is an argument comprehensible to anyone who wants you to cancel your vacation for anything less than bankruptcy, dissolution, or a big promotion.

Who Pays? You do, unless he insists or enjoys truly superior plastic. You could go Dutch, too, like friends do. In extremely complicated relationships, one party has been known to pay the tip while the other shouldered the Retsina and cheese. But in a situation fraught with interpersonal dynamics, rational thought poops out. Better to go with your gut. If your gut feels like paying, stoked as it is with pastrami and cream soda, cough up the fee. If it doesn't, prate and cackle like a cheerful jerk until the other guy is forced to say, "Hey! Lookie here!" and pick up the check.

Winning is great for people who believe they are playing a game. Quite a few do, mostly salespeople of various sizes and descriptions. A game is a structured activity, defined by rules, determined probabilities, and skill. The world of business, on the other hand, is an arbitrary pageant of rampaging human folly and grandeur. All central decisions—to buy, to sell, to create, to destroy—are, at the moment of their birth, irrational, visceral, a leap into the void. Don't play to win. Play to make something grow.

Workaholics, up to a certain point, must be pitied, for they are the prototypical victims of their own success. Hunching over charts or pumping paws into the wee hours, they exist without friends, family, or ideas about anything but business. They do not work because they love work, no matter how hard they try to tell you differently or guilt you into the same nutsy schedule. They work because they *must* work, because work is their home, and their loved one, and the only place they feel truly themselves. For some, it's a solitary life. Others get very, very lonely, and need troops around when they go over the fourth-quarter results for the fifteenth time at 7:30 P.M., when you have theater tickets. Such people must be trained. Immediately institute a rigorous program of punctuality. In by 8:30 A.M., out by 5:20. That's a long enough day for the corporation. If you have to fight for reasonable hours, do. You have a right to live a human life and make money at the same time.

Perhaps, on the other hand, you're a workaholic yourself, in which case, save yourself. Get a wife or husband to annoy, or a dimpled little baby to provide a wallop of perspective. It's never too late to join the human race, especially for you. After all, if you were a real workaholic, you wouldn't be reading this book. You'd be doing something compulsive.

X-Factor is the force of the unknown, and it walks beside you wherever you go. When snow grounds the Lear jet carrying the executive council on the way to your sales presentation, the X-factor has struck. When the mail-room guy spills coffee on your mass communication and you have to do it over in ten minutes, there it goes again. You can't act against it, because it has no shape until it's too late. All you can do is tear into it and repair the damage. You will. The X can hurt, but it can't destroy unless you turn tail and run.

Y

Yelling, indulged in more than once every several months, is an obnoxious and ineffective way of doing business. There are times when a good shriek is entirely appropriate, especially if you direct it at a wall, or a friend. Barking into a phone can even be forgiven by people who know it's just your wicked ways, nothing personal. But a noisome blast in some poor schlub's face for nothing more than bringing bad news, or typing too slowly, or being stupid, or vague, or lazy, only makes him scamper when the heat is on. Later, when he remembers the fact he was yelled at (for no reason, in his opinion), his resentment will grow, and his work will become minimalist, rather than generous. Motivation by fear is a management style more honored in the breach than the observance. Sure, it works. So does treating a person nice.

Unless, of course, you've tried that. In that case yelling is good. Okay, it only works in the short run, and pretty soon you'll have to turn to it again, and yet again, until it has become the basis of your entire miserable relationship. You scream, he jumps. Later he is morose, wounded. This hangdog act further goads you. Now you are ready to yell all the time. This makes you guilty. More anger. You begin taking alternative routes to

157

the men's room to avoid his door. The air is heavy with reproach. At that point, fire him before he turns you into a more outstanding jerk than he.

If, by the way, you find yourself yelling at more than one individual—your secretary one day, a fellow vice-president the next—the problem is with you, buddy. Don't be surprised when you feel your ears burning. People are probably somewhere in the building, yelling about you behind closed doors.

Yes Man is a viable occupation for extremely weak guys with no ideas. They attach themselves to extremely powerful guys with a few. The art is complex, not a shallow recitation of simple oohs, ahs, and an occasional "Outstanding, Doug!" On the contrary, effective yesmanship employs a welter of tools:

• *Ooh, Ah, and "Outstanding, Doug!":* Never forget the basics.

• *"Very Interesting . . .":* The ultimate noncommittal answer is one that sounds like warm agreement, when delivered with éclat.

• *Outright Flattery:* Guys who require incessant agreement like to have their grandiosity cleaned and waxed every hundred miles or so. It might be something simple like, "Gosh, Ron, you are the world's greatest people person," to the more ornate, "Sid, for a guy who knows his own mind you're amazingly willing to listen to feedback." Whatever he wants to hear. He must then treat you with a new respect. After all, if you're a jerk, of what value is all that lovely flattery?

• *Paranoia:* The flip side of needing to be right all the time is the conviction that you're never right. The accomplished yes man feeds that insecurity in his master, fertilizing it with incisive, nasty speculation, watering it with malicious rumor, pruning it with an occasional dash of happy news. The object is to convince him you're the only one in the entire organization with his interest at heart, the only one he can trust.

If you are, he's in trouble. A yes man is a traitor to the concept of good servitude. Sometimes a little disagreement is what an executive groping in a thicket of options needs to hear.

Z

Z's are nothing to be ashamed of. Sometimes you need a nap and work better after one. If your poker game went on a little late the night before, or you just endured a three-hour meeting on the relationship between long-term revenue and the incremental tax rate, or you have a monster night of spread sheets and argument before you, a quick retreat into dreamworld can hit the spot. The corporation gives you at least one hour for lunch. If you're an exec, even more. Of course, you don't get to take it every day, but that time is yours for the spending, or the wasting. Instead of that two-hour luncheon with the consultant-on-the-make, you have every right to lock your door, kick your feet up on the desk, toss your arm over your eyes, and hold your calls.

Do not, of course, take both lunch and a snooze, unless you have no work to do whatsoever. And after your winks, slap your face smartly, go directly, unobserved, to the men's room, and comb yourself. You don't want to stumble into your next meeting with your eyes all rheumy and your hair funneled into a pointy cone at the top of your head.

Zoo is a comfortable prison in which a variety of exotic and incompatible species are housed after they have exchanged their freedom for security. Lions stop roaring after a while and sleep far too much. Elephants are scratched and wheedled by a host of tiny keepers. Hyenas laugh at inane jokes of their own devising. Snakes digest mice slowly. Apes play, chase each other over toys and dead stumps in their circumscribed terrain. Wolves howl. Babies are born, old folks die. Above and around, the zoo goes on, staffed and restocked by invisible wardens.

After a while, thankfully, an animal simply forgets it's in a zoo at all, and thinks, "Hey, I've got my own crib. I'm eating pretty good. This must be real life." It's not, of course. But maybe it's better. After you get used to it, a well-run zoo is a lot more tolerable than a jungle.